Academic Science
Higher Education
and the
Federal Government
1950–1983

Academic Science
Higher Education
and the
Federal Government
1950–1983

John T. Wilson

The University of Chicago Press
Chicago and London

This essay was originally prepared as part
of the seminar "Higher Education and the Federal
Government," Department of Education, University of
Chicago, Spring Quarter, 1983. Both the seminar and
the work represented by the essay have been
generously supported by the Spencer Foundation and
by the Joseph and Helen Regenstein Foundation.

The University of Chicago Press, Chicago 60637
The University of Chicago Press, Ltd., London

Library of Congress Cataloging in Publication Data

Wilson, John T. (John Todd), 1914–
    Academic science, higher education, and the federal
government, 1950–1983.

    "This essay was originally prepared as part of the
seminar 'Higher Education and the Federal Government,'
Department of Education, University of Chicago, Spring
Quarter, 1983"—T.p. verso.
    1. Science and state—United States—History.
2. Higher education and state—United States—History.
I. Title.
Q127.U6W534 1983   353.0085'5'09   83-17964
ISBN 0-226-90051-7 (cloth)
        0-226-90052-5 (paper)

Contents

Preface

From time to time I have written essays on the state of federal government relations with higher education. The first of these was published under the title "Higher Education and the Washington Scene: 1963" in a special issue of the *Educational Record* 44, no. 2 (April 1963). The second appeared in *Minerva* 9, no. 2 (April 1971), and was titled "A Dilemma of American Science and Higher Educational Policy: The Support of Individuals and Fields versus the Support of Universities." Last year I published a third piece, "Higher Education and the Washington Scene: 1982." It was originally prepared for a graduate seminar as a summary paper describing the impact of Reagan administration policies on higher education programs. These three papers provided the basis for this essay.

In my judgment, the election of Ronald Reagan as president signaled the end of an era in the history of federal government relations with higher education that began as we approached the close of World War II. The era was characterized at its beginning by the conception of extremely productive programs for the support of academic science that had roots in the wartime involvement of college and university scientists in various efforts that utilized their intellectual resources. These federal government–academic science engagements continued in academic settings after the war in a variety of forms and under various agency and program auspices. They were eventually supplemented, after a terrible scare by the Russians and after some getting used to the idea, by federal government support for higher education functions per se, again in a variety of forms and under various auspices.

The Reagan administration initiated a fundamental change of course in economic and political directions which has, as a part of the change, significantly affected the relationships between the federal government and higher education. The change seems to me to require, on the part of those responsible for higher education, a consideration of fresh concepts and fresh approaches to federal support of higher education. It would be profitable at this time to step back and ask what we have learned from thirty years experience that might be modified in form and substance to serve both the interests of the nation and those of higher education on a permanent basis. What out of the post–World War II relationships between government and higher education should we have or could we have created that would rival, for example, the land-grant institution of the 1860s?

Despite the recent environment of suspicion and confrontation between the government and higher education, a large part of the post–World War II interaction has been a challenging and intellectually rewarding experience. Far more frequently than not, the two parties engaged in a mutually supportive effort that was intended to, and usually did, further the general welfare. That the engagement proceeded somewhat amateurishly at times is not surprising. Many of the problems were new and had little precedent in form or substance. That the interaction should have been allowed to deteriorate from a rather idealistic start to one of high suspicion and distrust constitutes a significant disservice on the part of both parties to the nation.

Within the foregoing context and in preparation for my 1982–83 seminar on higher education and the federal government, I drafted this essay covering the period 1950–83, highlighting the events that seem to me to convey a sense of the movement in policy and program development that has influenced relationships between the two parties since World War II. Also among its purposes is to further the idea that issues and problems have histories and that there may be a profit in knowing about these histories. Out of all of this, the question arises as to the possibility that there might be constructed a somewhat more rational, systematic relationship, reflecting values that are perceived as being fundamental to our society in the latter part of the twentieth century and based upon time cycles that are appropriate to the functions being supported. ("Appropriate," in this context, recalls in a larger historical sense, that higher education is much more closely related to the institution of the Church than it is to the institution of government.)

In the preparation of this piece I have borrowed as I considered the material pertinent from previous essays, especially from my most recent paper on the impact of the Reagan administration on higher education. I have also benefited from the wisdom and advice of two former colleagues in the National Science Foundation, Mrs. Mildred C. Allen and Mrs. Bertha Rubenstein.

1

Academic Science

The National Science Foundation

The Post–World War II Transition

The Constitution of the United States, in Article I, Section 8, empowered the Congress "to promote the progress of science . . . by securing to authors and inventors the exclusive right to their respective writings and discoveries," but for a limited time only. The initiation of a more systematic federal government policy for the support of academic science awaited the enactment of the Land Grant College legislation, some three-quarters of a century later. While limited both in the definition of the fields of science and the character of scientific work to be pursued, this and subsequent legislation established one model for cooperation between the federal government and colleges and universities for the promotion of scientific research.[1]

The forms of support which evolved following World War II derived essentially from the legislative authority and admin-

1. For a history of policies and activities of the federal government in science to 1940, see A. H. Dupree, *Science in the Federal Government* (Cambridge: Harvard University Press, 1957). For a history of legislation relating to the land-grant colleges and universities, see G. N. Rainsford, *Congress and Higher Education in the Nineteenth Century* (Knoxville: University of Tennessee Press, 1972). For an account of a failed attempt to legislate federal support for engineering and physical science in an academic setting which previewed many of the disagreements that marked debates within the academic community in the post–World War II period, see D. J. Kevles, "Federal Legislation for Engineering Experiment Stations: The Episode of World War I" *Technology and Culture* 12, no. 2 (April 1971): 182–89.

istrative policies of those agencies which assumed the responsibility for wartime contracts of the Office of Scientific Research and Development. The military, first through the War and Navy Departments and later through the Research and Development Board of the Department of Defense, maintained contact with civilian scientists returning to the universities, largely through adaptations of the contract system developed by the Office of Scientific Research and Development. The Office of Naval Research, particularly, not only provided for the needs of its own service, but in addition developed a highly regarded basic research program which later served as a model for the National Science Foundation. While also relying extensively on contracts to support research in universities, the Atomic Energy Commission introduced a different form of support by creating national laboratories through contracts with private corporations and, in some instances, with universities. The Public Health Service, which assumed responsibility for the contracts of the wartime Committee on Medical Research, greatly expanded its research branch, the National Institutes of Health, and through it sponsored a newly authorized government grant program in support of research, principally in the medical schools. Collectively, these developments set the patterns for government-university relationships in science prior to the establishment in 1950 of the National Science Foundation.[2]

The National Science Foundation

The legislation which created the National Science Foundation introduced an important new concept into the support of science by the federal government. In addition to creating a framework for subsidizing basic research, the National Science Foundation Act directed the foundation "to develop and encourage the pursuit of a national policy for the promotion of basic research and education in the sciences." The foundation was given full "authority, within the limits of available

2. For the genesis of the National Science Foundation, see Vannevar Bush, *Science: The Endless Frontier* (1945; reprinted by the National Science Foundation, May 1980).

appropriations to do all things necessary to carry out the provisions of this Act."[3]

The establishment of the National Science Foundation in the form embodied in the NSF Act of 1950 in itself constituted an important statement in setting the direction of national science policy. The debate on the issue of how the federal government should go about supporting academic science, if indeed it should do so at all during peacetime, had begun early in World War II. It was sparked by the concerns of a number of individuals over the perceived dominance of a limited number of large corporations in defense research which were also perceived as having close ties to a limited number of major research universities. These concerns prompted the introduction in 1942 of legislation sponsored by Senator Harley Kilgore of West Virginia to create a National Science Foundation.

Senator Kilgore's views as to how federal government support of science could best serve the public welfare were populist, encompassing programs of both fundamental and applied science, including social science, pertinent to the nation's social and economic needs. While protecting the intellectual freedom of the scientists whose work would be supported, the programs would be also responsive to the American political system, including a formula for geographic distribution of funds. The competing view contained in Vannevar Bush's now legendary report, *Science: The Endless Frontier,* favored procedures and forms for support of research which were more elitist in character, much along the traditional lines of the Rockefeller Foundation. While they differed in many respects, the essential factor that distinguished the Kilgore and the Bush concepts in terms of national policy is described by Daniel J. Kevles as boiling down to one basic issue:

Kilgore wanted a foundation responsive to lay control and prepared to support research for the advancement

3. National Science Foundation Act of 1950 (81st Congress, P.L. 507) as amended. The language of the act, as it relates to policy formulation, states that "the Board and the Director shall recommend and encourage the pursuit of national policies for the promotion of basic research and education in the sciences" (sec. 3[d]).

of the general welfare; Bush and his colleagues wanted
an agency run by scientists mainly for the purpose of
advancing science.[4]

In addition to the responsibility for developing national science policy, the "authorities" granted by law to the National
Science Foundation included initiation and support of basic
research in the mathematical, physical, medical, biological,
engineering, and other sciences; the awarding of scholarships
and fellowships in these same areas; the exchange of scientific
information; the evaluation of the scientific research programs
of other government agencies and the correlation of the foundation's programs with those of other agencies, both public
and private; and the maintenance of a register and clearing
house for information regarding scientific and technical personnel. There was also a function relating to support of research on the national defense to be exercised at the request
of the secretary of defense. This was not pursued.

The National Science Foundation Act defined the foundation
institutionally as consisting of "a National Science Board and
a Director." As prescribed by the act, board members were to
be persons "eminent in the fields of the basic sciences, medical
science, engineering, agriculture, education, or public affairs,
. . . selected solely on the basis of established records of distinguished service . . . and . . . so selected as to provide representation of the views of scientific leaders in all areas of the
Nation."[5]

4. For a history of the debate over post–World War II science policy see
D. J. Kevles, "The National Science Foundation and the Debate over Postwar
Research Policy, 1942–1945," *Isis* 68, no. 241 (1977): 5–26 (quote from p. 16).
See also "Memorandum of Disapproval of the National Science Foundation
Bill," 6 August 1947, in *Public Papers of the President* (Washington, D.C.:
U.S. Government Printing Office, 1947), 368–71, in which President Truman
vetoed an earlier National Science Foundation bill on the grounds that it vested
too much power in the National Science Board to determine policies and to
control expenditures outside the constitutional authority of the president.

For a discussion of some historic failures reflecting the political issues involved in the development of a national science policy, see D. K. Price, "Federal Money and University Research," *Science,* 21 January 1966, 285–90.

5. NSF Act of 1950. For a detailed discussion of events surrounding the
appointment of the first National Science Board and the director, see J. M.
England, *A Patron for Pure Science: The National Science Foundation's For-*

The appointment of the first National Science Board and the director were events of fundamental importance for the foundation. They would not only reflect the basic definition of the new agency but they would establish for the future, as a safeguard for the foundation under changing political administrations, the tone and qualitative characteristics of the institution that was assigned responsibility for national science policies. To balance various and potentially conflicting interests such as those of research scientists, university administrators, and public and private and large and small institutions, the legislation required that the president consider recommendations for board membership from a wide range of constituencies. These included, for example, the National Academy of Sciences, the scientific societies, and "other scientific or educational organizations." Although not required by law, recommendations for the board were also sought by the White House within government, from the Bureau of the Budget, the Civil Service Commission, and the Interdepartmental Committee on Scientific Research and Development.

Rumors reinforced concerns within the academic and scientific communities that political considerations might intervene in the selection of board members. But as matters turned out, the first National Science Board satisfied, in a very reasonable way, qualitative criteria, institutional representation, and other "political" considerations, including color, sex, religion, and geographical distribution.[6] Twenty of twenty-four

mative Years, 1945–1957 (Washington, D.C.: National Science Foundation, 1982), chap. 6.

6. The membership of the original National Science Board consisted of Sophie D. Aberle, research director, University of New Mexico; Chester I. Barnard, president, Rockefeller Foundation; Robert P. Barnes, head, Department of Chemistry, Howard University; Detlev W. Bronk, president, Johns Hopkins University and National Academy of Sciences; Gerty T. Cori, professor of biological chemistry, Washington University; James B. Conant, president, Harvard University; John W. Davis, president, West Virginia State College; Charles Dollard, president, Carnegie Corporation; Lee A. DuBridge, president, California Institute of Technology; Edwin B. Fred, president, University of Wisconsin; Paul M. Gross, vice-president, Duke University; George D. Humphrey, president, University of Wyoming; O. W. Hyman, dean of the Medical School, University of Tennessee; Robert F. Loeb, professor of medicine, College of Physicians and Surgeons, Columbia University; Donald H. Mc-

members had college and university ties, which virtually guaranteed sympathetic relationships with institutions of higher
learning. Representation from private universities outweighed
representation from public, and only two schools were not
involved in graduate education. Six members were university
presidents and another had been a president of a black college
for many years. Nine members had backgrounds in the biological and medical sciences and nine had backgrounds in physical and engineering areas, including mathematics. Social science
was represented by two board members. On other dimensions,
there were two women, two blacks, two Catholics, and two
from private industry. One of the two women, Dr. Gerty Cori,
held the distinction of being a Nobel laureate.

Prior to the appointment of the board, there were some who
feared that the major East and West Coast research universities
would dominate the group, thus biasing the foundation toward
their interests. But these fears proved to be unfounded. However, there were other connections which did forcefully influence the direction and the tone of the board's considerations.
Eight of the twenty-four board members were also members
of the National Academy of Sciences. In addition, four of these
eight had ties through trusteeship or senior advisory roles in
two Rockefeller institutions, the Rockefeller Foundation and
the Rockefeller Research Institute (now Rockefeller University). This group of eight represented a nucleus of like-minded
individuals within the board, whose views strongly coincided
with Vannevar Bush's conception of the foundation.

In regard to the appointment of the foundation's first director,
the legislation gave the board the responsibility of recommending candidates to the president. More important, the act
forbade the appointment of a director before the board had an

opportunity to make its recommendations. There were the usual rumors about the president's choice for the head of the foundation, and there is some evidence that President Truman's first choice, although a distinguished public figure in his own right, would not have met with board endorsement. But the president made other arrangements for him and, after reviewing the list of nominees presented by the National Science Board, appointed from the list as the foundation's first director Alan T. Waterman, chief scientist of the Office of Naval Research. It was a logical and widely acclaimed choice. It satisfied a number of critical conditions: The president had an able administrator with experience in government affairs to head up the new agency; the board had a scientist whose integrity was unchallenged and who, as well as having prewar academic credentials from Yale, had grown up with postwar developments between government and academic science; the academic community could be reassured by the fact that the director had shown sympathetic understanding of its needs in developing the basic research program of ONR, which, indeed, served as the surrogate for the foundation during the latter's long gestation period.

Thus, the foundation as defined both by legislation and by President Truman's appointments of board members and director could be viewed as a fundamental science policy triumph, especially an academic science policy triumph, for those who identified with the view that governmental decisions regarding science and its institutions should be made essentially according to the judgments of the leaders in the scientific and academic communities. Those who felt that governmental decisions regarding support of science should, like other public policy decisions, be a function of more-traditional democratic political processes would have to await another day to reassert their views.

Establishing Program Priorities

From the beginning, two quite different motivating forces were in conflict in shaping the behavior of the foundation. On the one hand, the Bureau of the Budget's interest in the establishment of the foundation had been to create an agency that would essentially be its handmaiden in serving the executive office of the president. In this concept, the policy formulation and evaluation functions were uppermost in the minds of BOB staff, and it was in this direction that bureau actions attempted to shape the foundation's development.

On the other hand, and of far greater relevance to institutions of higher learning, the National Science Board, dominated by academic administrators and scientists, viewed as more important those functions having to do with the support of academic research and graduate education. As the board and the director began to frame and initiate the activities of the foundation, priority was given to the support and advancement of basic research and to the education and training of prospective scientists. In the first annual report of the foundation, the judgment of the board regarding the pursuit of "coordinated" national science policies, including academic science policy, was that such an endeavor should be approached with care and that it would take some time.[7]

The problems facing the new director and the board reflected a mixture of substantive judgments and bureaucratic requirements. Almost immediately, program priorities had to be translated into budget categories and defensible estimates of monetary needs which, taken together, would represent the agency's budget. The budget would be defended before those responsible for the president's overall budget, namely, BOB officials, who in so doing would switch roles from godfather to prosecutor, and before the House and Senate appropriations committees. Programs also had to be considered from the viewpoint of other executive branch agencies whose activities paralleled, overlapped, or were tangentially related to the foundation.

Although such matters are of more historical than policy interest, it was not inconsequential to the universities how the National Science Foundation would resolve interagency issues:

7. *First Annual Report of the National Science Foundation, 1950–51* (Washington, D.C.: U.S. Government Printing Office, 1951).

for example, whether fellowship programs would continue under the auspices of the Atomic Energy Commission and the National Institutes of Health, and whether the foundation's research support programs would be new and self-initiated or be transferred from other research supporting agencies, or whether they would merely "fill the gaps" left by the other agencies.

The arena within which substantive problems and priorities were settled was budget negotiation between the foundation and the Bureau of the Budget. This, of course, was influenced by the outcome of discussions between the director and the board and between the director and representatives of various executive branch agencies having science programs. Out of these negotiations emerged the foundation's first operating budget. The appropriation of $3.5 million for 1952, although small and not received by the foundation until well into that fiscal year, was sufficient to initiate programs of the foundation's own choosing and to give its staff the experience of translating the theory of program formulation into program operation. As for policy formulation, the foundation was successful in persuading the bureau that the best approach to national science policy was through comprehensive surveys of support of science by government, industry, and educational institutions.[8] With the support of the board, the director evaded the issue of program evaluation of other government agencies.

Although the fellowship program was the first to be announced by the foundation, it was the support of basic research, almost exclusively within university and college settings, that established and cemented the foundation's relationships with the higher education community. In an announcement of December 1951, it was indicated that reseach support would encompass all of the fields within the physical, mathematical, engineering, biological, and nonclinical medical sciences.[9] The

8. The original series from the program was Federal Funds for Science, which, with various subsequent title changes, is now in its fourth decade of publication.

9. Grants for Scientific Research: A Guide for the Submission of Research Proposals (Washington, D.C.: National Science Foundation, 1951).

social sciences, eligible for support only as "other sciences" in the foundation's authorizing legislation, were conceived during these early years as being adjunct to the natural science programs, falling under such rubrics as "psychobiology," "anthropology and related sciences," and "sociophysical sciences." It was not until 1958 that the Office of Social Sciences was administratively established, offering support for research in anthropology, economics, linguistics, history and philosophy of science, demography, and social psychology. Legislative establishment of the social sciences as an area eligible for support would await a major amendment to the National Science Foundation Act in 1968.[10]

As chief scientist in the Office of Naval Research, Alan Waterman had developed a highly professional staff of scientists for the administration of that organization's basic research program. With the announcement of his appointment as the first director of the National Science Foundation a number of his former staff within the biological science group, who had been following the fate of NSF legislation with more than passing interest, indicated their desire to join him at the foundation. This group was augmented quickly by recruitment of staff from the academic community.[11]

10. Federal support of the social sciences constitutes a continuing saga. Pertinent readings include, among many other sources, F. R. Harris, "Political Science and the Proposal for a National Social Science Foundation," *American Political Science Review* 61, no. 4 (1967): 1088–95. For an example of a "special commission" study, see the report of the Special Commission on the Social Sciences of the National Science Board, *Knowledge into Action: Improving the Nation's Use of the Social Sciences* (Washington, D.C.: U.S. Government Printing Office, 1969). See also Harold Orlans, "Social Science Research Policies in the United States," *Minerva* 9 (1971): 7–31. For the latest, but almost certainly not the last in a series of special reports on the social sciences see National Academy of Sciences, *Behavioral and Social Sciences: National Resources* (Washington, D.C.: National Academy Press, 1982).

11. The legislative authority for the foundation exempted it from civil service rules which traditionally bound older agencies like the Department of Agriculture and the Office of Education. This freedom permitted the recruitment of university scientists to assist in the creation and administration of its programs. The rotation in and out of university scientists in the early years of the foundation resulted in a better understanding of the problems of the federal government among the scientists and of academic institutions among NSF staff.

As a result, the foundation had a running start in the administration of its research support program. Consequently, at its meeting on 1 February 1952, less than two months following the mailing of the guide for proposal submission, the first foundation research grants, all in the biological and medical sciences, received board approval. Thus by a series of events including receipt of proposals, evaluation by a screening panel of experts in the particular fields of science, review by a "divisional committee" to ensure adherence to "policies" of the division, review by the director's office, and final approval by the National Science Board, a connection that was to be fertile and productive in the support of basic research was established between the neophyte agency and the nation's colleges and universities. The physical science research programs got underway shortly thereafter and broadened the foundation's connections across the natural science spectrum. By 1958, with the emergence of the social science research program per se, foundation research support essentially reached the full academic science spectrum.

For an agency whose budget has recently passed the billion dollar level, the foundation's early appropriations seem meagre indeed. However, the shortage of funds did have some advantages. The staff had time to discuss the merits of various program concepts, to visit university laboratories, and to debate at length appropriate policies that would make the foundation "different" from the typical government agency. In the years between 1952 and 1958, obligations for basic research grants slowly rose from somewhat over $1 million in 1952 for both major divisions to about $18 million in 1958.[12] The biological and physical sciences groups maintained essentially equal support levels throughout the period until the support of research facilities inevitably tipped the balance of funding toward the physical sciences. When the Office of Social Sciences was established, obligations for that area were $.3 million, and doubled to $.6 million in 1958.

12. Total foundation obligations rose from $3.5 million to $50 million during the 1952–58 period.

As appropriations increased, research support was broadened to cover funding for physical facilities and for major equipment for the conduct of research, both within the universities and in independent research units, generally "national laboratories" managed by consortia composed of associations of major research universities. This latter concept led to the early establishment of the National Radio Astronomy Observatory at Green Bank, West Virginia, and the Kitt Peak National Observatory near Tucson, Arizona. These were followed by a third astronomical observatory at Cerro Tololo, Chile, and an atmospheric research laboratory at Boulder, Colorado. Other examples of major facility support included biological field stations, construction of oceanographic research vessels, university computing facilities, nuclear research equipment, and specialized university research laboratories of various kinds.

By the later 1950s, the foundation was involved in supporting and coordinating for the whole federal government the United States' participation in the International Geophysical Year. This was one of the foundation's most successful ventures in large-scale science, and as an outgrowth, a major international cooperative research effort in Antarctica continued under NSF auspices. Other ventures in "big science" were not always so successful, and in the 1960s the foundation experienced a major failure in a venture to drill into the deep interior of the earth and take samples of cores from beneath the earth's mantle (popularly known as Project Mohole). But success and failure aside, from the very beginning the foundation clearly established itself as a supporter of first-rate scientific research, with programs and under conditions that both gained and warranted the respect of the university scientific community. Despite some intrusion by policy considerations under the Johnson administration (1965), which required that the strengthening of the country's institutional base be taken into consideration by all agencies supporting scientific research (of which more later), the foundation's research support programs established and maintained high standards and have generally and consistently been viewed within the academic science community as being devoted to excellence.

Although the board had hoped to initiate a fellowship program on a "pilot plan" basis as early as January 1951, delays in appropriations prevented it. A planned program of some two thousand fellowships for fiscal 1952 had to be reduced sharply because of limited funds. In addition to funding difficulties, differences within the board over what constituted appropriate stipends and other allowances complicated the program's development. But with the differences eventually resolved, the foundation in November of 1951 announced the fellowship program and made arrangements with the National Research Council of the National Academy of Sciences to do the initial screening of applications. The foundation made final decisions for its first awards of predoctoral and postdoctoral fellowships in April 1952.

In theory the fellowship program was to attract bright young students into scientific careers in response to a national shortage in scientific and engineering personnel. It was hoped that the fellowship would distinguish its recipients without being disruptive to university policies or the policies that governed other federal fellowship programs. It was agreed by the board that more first-year awards should be made to attract college seniors into scientific careers, and that initial stipends should be substantial and incremental in second- and third-year awards. Fellowships would be for full-time study and would carry living and family allowances, as well as tuition payment, all of which the foundation expected would be tax exempt.

Initial awards encompassed predoctoral fellowships and both senior and recent postdoctorals in the fields of mathematical, biological, physical, medical, and engineering sciences. Recipients had to be United States citizens and were required to submit the loyalty oath and the affidavit required by the NSF Act. Applications did not follow the theory of first-year awards, and the distribution pattern of awards had an essentially equal number of first- and second-year, and a predominance of third-year fellows.

With time the foundation broadened its original conception of the fellowship program. Starting in fiscal year 1956, programs for senior faculty scientists and for undergraduate college faculty were initiated. By the end of 1957, responding to growing pressures from complaints that predoctoral fellows were choosing a limited number of schools to pursue graduate study, the foundation created "cooperative graduate fellowships." These were awarded to graduate students in situ, at a wide range of universities having graduate training programs in the sciences and engineering. Eventually, the spectrum of the fellowship program was broadened in substance to encompass the social sciences, and starting in 1958, the fellowship program made awards to the areas of the social sciences supported by the research program.

While the foundation's fellowship programs did not dominate the federal government's support efforts, the very high selection standards in NSF programs did set it apart and did attract national interest. An important "secondary gain" was achieved through the publication of "honorable mention" lists of individuals who were thus identified and supported by other fellowship programs. The foundation did not exercise its authority to support undergraduate scholarships on the basis of a decision that it was not in the national interest to offer federal scholarships to undergraduates who wished to become scientists so long as similar support was not available to other undergraduates.

Beyond the fellowship programs, the foundation's support of science education in other forms developed slowly. This was in part a function of the small budget, which would have precluded any undertaking of significant size. But it also stemmed from a belief on the part of the foundation's legal office that authority was lacking for support of such activities on other than an "experimental" basis to further the foundation's policy responsibilities. Within the board and among the senior staff, there were strong feelings that any federal government role in science education, especially at the secondary school level, belonged to the Office of Education. The chairman of the board was firmly opposed to asking for amendments to the foundation's legislative authority that would permit programmatic entry into this area.

Despite conservatism at higher levels, education program directors and their advisory groups pushed with some success toward secondary school science education. Studies aimed at identifying bright high-school students and at ways of motivating them to consider science careers were initiated. A program of traveling libraries to smaller high schools was launched, along with a program to explore the use of training films to teach secondary school science.

Outside the foundation, a White House Conference on Education held in the autumn of 1955 reflected a national attitude that was moving in the direction of increased federal government aid for the nation's public schools. Undoubtedly influenced by the changing national mood, but also stimulated by pressure from the Committee on Scientists and Engineers that had been established by the Office of Defense Mobilization, the director of the foundation advocated in a December speech to the Association for the Advancement of Science a more active role for the foundation in science education. The support of teacher institutes (whose success had already been demonstrated by sponsors in the industrial and private foundation world) seemed to be the most promising direction. The foundation, at the request of the Mathematical Association of America, had partially supported in the summer of 1953, an institute at the University of Colorado for college teachers of mathematics. An institute for college-level teachers of physics also was partially supported that same year, under the sponsorship of the University of Minnesota. Four institutes for college teachers and an "experimental" institute for high-school mathematics teachers were supported during the summer of 1954. Over the next two years, the number of institutes increased steadily. With rising concern for the position of the United States vis-à-vis Russia in science education at the secondary school level, the foundation proposed for fiscal year 1957 a significant increase in the budget for science education, but met with little success within the Bureau of the Budget.

By the time the budget reached the Congress, the chairman of the foundation's appropriation subcommittee, Mr. Albert Thomas of Texas, had become more than ordinarily interested in this aspect of the foundation's programs. Stimulated by Nicholas DeWitt's recently published book *Soviet Professional Manpower,* Mr. Thomas raised the question with foundation staff as to whether the foundation should be paying more attention to the education of high-school teachers of science.

The query caused considerable consternation within the foundation. Not only was there a question regarding the legal authority of the foundation to support high-school teacher training, but there were also potential problems regarding relationships with the Office of Education should the foundation do so. Moreover, the priorities of the foundation did not place high-school science, or the training of high-school teachers of science, at a very high level.

In the exchange of views between the foundation and Congress, Mr. Thomas and his subcommittee held their position. The foundation's appropriation for fiscal year 1957 carried the stipulation that no less than $9.5 million from the total appropriation of $40 million (as compared to $1.3 million from a total of $16 million in the year before) be obligated for supplementary training in science for high-school teachers. This action contained two early and important lessons for the foundation: the power of the Congress to determine through budget action the course of academic science policy and the difference between Congress and the foundation with respect to program priorities to benefit the needs of the nation.

Other science education programs developed and supported by the foundation took the form of course-content and curricular revision. These ranged from relatively small-scale efforts to massive national programs to revise the content of courses in physics, mathematics, chemistry, and biology.[13] Early attempts also were made to enhance public understanding of science, especially science as related to public policy issues. If one considers the fellowship programs as having been conceived with the intention of supporting individuals who were

13. For a review and evaluation of the science education movement, especially curricular reform, see P. W. Jackson, "The Reform of Science Education in Public Schools: A Cautionary Tale." *Daedalus* 112, no. 2 (Spring 1983): 143–66.

potentially the most talented scientists, the other science education programs may be said to have attempted the most direct effort in the country's history to enhance science education on a very broad spectrum and on a wide range of levels.

Research and fellowship support, the national laboratories and national programs such as Antarctica, and the science education efforts were the major operating program activities from the time of the foundation's founding until the mid-1960s. Other programs during these years, which were of direct interest to higher education, included the National Register of Scientific and Technical Personnel and the Office of Science Information (the authority for which was included within the National Defense Education Act). The latter engaged in both research and administrative support programs covering storage and retrieval systems, mechanical translation, support for scientific publications, scientific data centers, and collection of foreign science information.

The support programs of the foundation were to be developed and administered with a view to enhancing the quality of academic science in the United States.[14] Although there was no explicit overall policy to shape them, the programs were directed toward three interrelated ends: (1) the advancement of science through the support of basic (and some applied) research, as well as through the support of physical plant facilities in universities; (2) the development of individuals, ranging from students in lower school systems through undergraduates to pre- and postdoctoral scholars in higher educational institutions; and (3) the development and support of national laboratories and national programs for conducting research and for education in science. Institutional support was avoided for a variety of reasons, including the fear of being accused of intrusion into institutional affairs, the invidiousness of making comparisons between institutions, and because of

14. See, for example, Subcommittee on Science, Research, and Development, House Committee on Science and Astronautics, *The National Science Foundation: A General Review of Its First Fifteen Years,* 89th Congress, 1st sess., 1966, which on page 125 notes the foundation's penchant for placing "quality ahead of quantity."

objections by individuals who were members of the board and
of foundation advisory groups.

The Pursuit of Policy: Lower Case "p"

A fundamental problem of a philosophical nature differentiated the conception of the foundation as it was established
from the populist conception inherent in the proposed Kilgore
legislation. As Dr. Philip Handler, in testimony before the House
Subcommittee on Science, Research, and Technology pointed
out, there was "built into the Foundation from time zero a
basic conflict as old as the Republic—egalitarianism versus
selective support of the very best of science that some hold to
be elitism."[15] There were, of course, strong precedents in favor
of the view that only the best of science should be supported:
the great private foundations; the record of the Office of Scientific Research and Development, which could not conceiv-
ably have followed any other course during wartime; and the
legislative history of the NSF Act which, among other things,
had rejected a proposed formula distribution in favor of merit
as the primary basis for awarding grants and fellowships.

The National Science Board resolved the conflict by deciding
on competitive and highly selective criteria to govern the operation of foundation programs. The board's view was reflected
in a statement of its first chairman, Dr. James Conant, in the
foundation's annual report for 1950–51: "In the advance of
science and its application to many practical problems, there
is no substitute for first-class men. Ten second-rate scientists
or engineers cannot do the work of one who is in the first
rank."[16]

As for how the foundation might best get on with supporting
science, the NSF Act permitted it almost unlimited imagination
in devising arrangements for carrying out its responsibilities.
After staff study and board consideration, the foundation elected

15. House of Representatives, *Hearings before the Subcommittee on Science, Research, and Technology of the Committee on Science and Technology,*
96th Congress, May 16, 17, September 11, 12, 13, 1979.
16. See the foreword to the *First Annual Report of the NSF.*

to use the so-called project method and the legal mechanism of the grant as the most appropriate way to underwrite the research activities authorized by its legislation.[17] Underlying this decision was the foundation's conception of its task as the support of talented individuals who had worthwhile ideas about what they wished to do and how to do it. The foundation had to satisfy itself only that the proposed work would contribute significantly to its field and that the individual had the intellectual capacity and the facilities available to him to conduct a sound and imaginative research program. No specific utility from the work was expected or sought. It was recognized above all that basic research could not be defined precisely, since the end result was unknown. Thus a more binding contractual form would be inappropriate. In no sense were activities supported by the foundation considered as being done "for the government."

From the point of view of program administration, the project method and utilization of the grant mechanism had significant advantages. Imaginatively interpreted and administered, it could be applied to research problems of an individual faculty member, but it was sufficiently flexible to encompass the work of a group in a broad area of science. It was ideal for taking advantage of newly developing disciplines, and it was acceptable for the support of "national programs." As utilized by the foundation, it called upon the advice of leading scientists in the evaluation of project proposals, and yet before a grant could be made, it required the endorsement of the faculty member's institution.

From a more strictly "administrative" viewpoint, the grant mechanism avoided the cumbersome controls and restrictions which were traditionally utilized by government programs to ensure that the government got what it had contracted for. These controls are many and varied, and to a large extent, they put the burden of proof on the contractor. They include such

17. See Office of the Secretary of the Board, National Science Foundation, *Administrative Aspects of Research Support* (Washington, D.C., 1951). Fellowship programs followed the traditional National Academy of Science practice of issuing individual awards in the form of renewable grants.

things as the initial justification of cost estimates, detailed accounting and record keeping to prove that expenditures are
properly connected with the work, records of all property acquired under the contract, justification of each request for a
"progress payment," and, ultimately, the closing of the contract under a detailed set of rules for accounting for funds,
disposition of residual property, delivery of reports, proto-
types, and so on.

The grant, in contrast, was deemed to limit the contractual
relationship to the definition of the general field in which the
work would be conducted. The grantee was free to determine
his course of action within that field. The budget of a proposal
for support was presented in broad categories and the investigator was free to change the amounts within budget categories
at his discretion once he received a grant. No accounting was
required for property acquired under the grant; property so
acquired belonged to the institution. Grants were paid in advance and a postaudit, if made at all, was to determine only
that the funds were spent for purposes of the grant. Thus, the
foundation's chosen mode of support was purposely designed
to relieve grantees of administrative burdens as much as
possible.[18]

But in the course of time, a variety of constraints arose,
including civil rights legislation, various patent regulations, and
"buy American" restrictions, which led to modification of grants
from essentially straightforward transfers of funds from the
public treasury to a form in which numerous administrative
restrictions were introduced. Among these, some were more
annoying than others and some were more intrusive than others
into the operations of the recipient institution. Without ques-

18. Foundation grants were paid in advance, allowed a uniform rate of indirect costs, permitted retention of equipment, paid publication costs, allowed
travel costs and retention of any patent, with royalty free license to the government. Grants were to be "administered" by a scientific officer of the foundation, but the "form" of the proposal was left largely to the applicant. Salary
payment for summer research was also allowed, but there were some problems
as to whether it should cover two-ninths or three-ninths of the academic year
salary of the principal investigators. "Released time" during the academic
year also was an allowable cost (ibid.).

tion, none was more troublesome and more resistant to mutually satisfactory solution between government and the higher education community than the "indirect costs" associated with the conduct of research.[19]

Indirect costs, sometimes referred to as "overhead," cover expenses of a university or other research institution that are not associated with a particular project, but which are esential to maintaining a library, for example, or for paying heating and lighting bills and otherwise maintaining the institution qua institution. Their importance in the context of formulating administrative policy for research support is essentially twofold: first whether they should be paid at all; second, if they are to be paid, should they be paid in full or only in part. If paid in full, this necessarily means detailed inquiry into the accounting procedures and practices of the grantee institution, as well as some procedure for relating the rate of indirect cost payment to salaries of personnel involved in the research, since such costs are usually determined as some percentage of salary expenditures. To get into this sort of administrative requirement meant vitiating the essence of the grant. To avoid this, the foundation, "for simplicity and ease of administration," chose to allow indirect costs at a uniform fixed rate of 15 percent of the total grant, which was estimated to be somewhat below "full" overhead costs.

This decision ran counter to a policy recommended by the American Council on Education, whose position was that all government agencies should pay "the full cost of research, including indirect or overhead expenses" according to a formula utilized by the military services, popularly known as the "Blue Book."[20]

Initial foundation policy differed from other government grant-making agencies. The National Institutes of Health then allowed but 8 percent indirect costs and the Atomic Energy Commission paid the same. In late 1954, in an attempt to create

19. For a detailed discussion of the early history of the indirect-cost controversy see England, *A Patron for Pure Science,* chaps. 9 and 15.
20. American Council on Education, *Sponsored Research Policy of Colleges and Universities* (Washington, D.C., 1954), 18.

some order in government research supporting programs (private foundations usually allowed no overhead costs), the Bureau of the Budget asked the National Science Foundation to recommend by 30 June 1955 a uniform policy on allowances for indirect costs in all federal research grant programs. The foundation's recommendation (arrived at only after lengthy and difficult inter- and intraagency negotiations and debate) was that all federal agencies supporting research grants be prepared to pay indirect costs at a rate determined by "Blue Book" principles, but that any institution should have an option of accepting an unaudited flat rate of 25 percent of the salaries included in a grant budget.

The flat-rate reimbursement concept was vigorously promoted within the foundation by program staff. Their view sought some reasonable compromise that would compensate institutions fairly, even though slightly below full cost, in the interests of avoiding the creation of a large auditing bureaucracy and the inevitable institutional cost, in the long run, of man hours spent haggling with auditors over disallowances and the composition of the formula upon which the indirect-cost reimbursement rate would be based. Although it was recognized that there would be some reluctance on the part of the General Accounting Office to accept the flat rate, there also was evidence that because of its advantages, this approach might be approved by the comptroller general if the case were to be adequately presented to him. Supporting this hope was the fact that the comptroller general had consented not to have NSF grants audited at all during the first few years of its existence.

There was equally vigorous opposition to the flat rate within the academic community, from the business officers' group and from presidents of institutions receiving large amounts of support from the Department of Defense. Generally, these individuals feared that if the flat-rate policy gained acceptance, it would threaten reimbursement of higher overhead rates by agencies supporting contract research. Some presidents were members of the National Science Board.[21]

21. Conflict of interest when academic scientists and administrators influenced policies and administrative actions on matters in which they were directly involved in their private capacities is nowhere better illustrated than in

It would be encouraging to report that eventually all parties saw the merit of the proposed flat rate for overhead reimbursement on basic research grants and that, as a result, endless hours of discussion and debate had thereby been avoided. Much money might also have been saved—unquestionably enough to support a considerable amount of research. But that is not the case. Discussions on overhead reimbursement dragged on within government and between government and university representatives. National Science Board minutes on the subject for October 1959 indicate that the board, by that time, saw "a glimmer of hope that the end might be near." But within this past academic year, *Science* magazine has published heated exchanges between faculty, university business officers, and government representatives over proposed revisions in Circular A-21.[22] After thirty-odd years, the end is not yet in sight.[23]

The issue of indirect costs and the failure to come to a resolution of it notwithstanding, the project system of research support was generally well received by working scientists.[24] Paradoxically, its very success generated two problems that in the early 1960s necessitated "corrections in course" within the system. The first stemmed from stress within institutions receiving increasing numbers of research project grants, the second from stress between institutions because of the uneven distribution of research funds.

---

the debate over indirect costs. The close relationship between the National Science Board and the National Academy of Sciences is another example. The problem was a matter of discomfort to many board members and to the staff of the foundation, particularly the Office of the General Counsel. Not infrequently one gained an impression that to some board members conflict of interest was a concept rooted in and having direct lineage to the doctrine of divine right of kings.

22. Office of Management and Budget, Circular A-21, "Principles for Determining Costs Applicable to Grants, Contracts, and Other Agreements with Educational Institutions" (Revised 1979).

23. "Can OMB Cure Accountability Strife?" *Science,* 10 December 1982, 1097.

24. The project grant pattern proved to be so successful that the Committee on Public Policy of the National Academy of Sciences states in its first report that "research project grants and contracts should remain the backbone of federal policy in support of basic research in science in the universities" *Federal Support of Basic Research in Institutions of Higher Learning* (Washington, D.C.: National Academy of Sciences, 1964), 1.

In an attempt to alleviate the rigidity of the project grant system and thus to allow some "free" funds to institutions which were experiencing the inflexibilities that project support creates, the National Science Foundation in 1961 and the National Institutes of Health in 1962 initiated "institutional grants for science" programs. The foundation's program was directed toward the institutions which had already received its grants. It retained the principle of quality discrimination in that the amount of the "institutional grant" was a function of the total amount of the funds awarded competitively to individual members of the institution through National Science Foundation grants. The National Institutes of Health program was directed toward "health professional schools" and used analogous criteria to award grants. Thus these two types of institutional grants did not aim to bring about a wider distribution of funds among the colleges and universities of the country.

The second problem, that of the stress between institutions caused by the uneven distribution of funds among them, proved to be a more difficult one to resolve and, as we shall later describe, led to the first serious review of the foundation by Congress since the foundation's establishment.

The Pursuit of Policy: Upper Case "P"

Despite the director's and the board's cautious and considered approach to science policy responsibilities, there was throughout the early 1950s continuing pressure on the foundation from the Bureau of the Budget to assume a more vigorous posture in science policymaking, particularly in relation to the programs of other government agencies. The bureau strongly desired the foundation to take on the responsibility for evaluating the various existing research support programs and to review the allocation of funds for these programs. The debate over this issue continued, with feeling at times. It eventually came to a denouement in 1954 with the issuance of Executive Order 10521 by President Eisenhower. In this order, the role of the foundation in policymaking was "clarified" and limited specifically to recommending "policies for the promotion and support of basic research and education in the sciences, including policies with respect to furnishing guidance toward defining the responsibilities of the Federal Government in the conduct and support of basic research."[25]

In response to Executive Order 10521, the foundation produced a series of policy studies on specific problems relating to academic research and science education, of direct interest to institutions of higher learning. These dealt, among other things, with federal financial support of physical facilities and major equipment for the conduct of research, strengthening basic research in the United States, and governmentwide practices with respect to title to equipment, travel costs, and other administrative aspects of research support.[26]

The report on physical facilities led eventually to legislation that permitted all agencies of the federal government to vest title to facilities and equipment in universities. The principal impact of the report on basic research was to validate what Sputnik (1957) was to dramatically demonstrate—the challenged position of the United States in world scientific leadership and the need for enhanced basic research support. The report on government-university relationships was a model for government agencies regarding principles and practices in their dealings with universities. More or less as a "first principle," the report recommended that research support should be dissociated from the financial needs of universities and not used

25. Executive Order 10521, 17 March 1954. See also, Executive Order 10807, 13 March 1959, which reinforced the assignment of basic research and science education policy responsibility to the foundation.

26. *Federal Financial Support of Physical Facilities and Major Equipment for the Conduct of Scientific Research,* June 1957; *Basic Research: A National Resource,* October 1957; and *Government-University Relationships in Federally Sponsored Research and Develpment,* April 1958. A description of these three studies, as well as other NSF reports bearing upon national science policy beyond the boundaries of academic science are contained in Philip M. Smith's excellent report *The National Science Board and the Formulation of National Science Policy,* NSB-81-440, 31 July 1981. Chapter 3 of the report describes several NSF case studies, for example: *Recommended Future Role of the Federal Government with Respect to Research in Synthetic Rubber,* 1955; *Weather and Climate Modification,* 1966; and *Weather Modification, Law, Controls, Operation,* 1966. See also England, *A Patron for Pure Science,* chap. 10.

as a subterfuge for federal aid to higher education per se. In addition, the report pointed out that the universities should be alert to the inherent dangers in such issues as accepting salary support for faculty from research grants, establishing applied research programs on otherwise academically oriented campuses, accepting "classified" research, and allowing themselves to be seduced by activities that reflected government interests rather than their own. Finally, the report recommended that all federal agencies be empowered to support academic research by grant as well as by contract.

What was perhaps the foundation's finest hour in regard to academic science policy occurred in early 1954. It was the period of the Army-McCarthy hearings, the security difficulties of Robert Oppenheimer with the Atomic Energy Commission, and a time when a national hysteria was overriding the country's sense of personal rights in political thought and action. The annual spring meetings of the National Academy of Sciences buzzed with rumors and allegations that a number of scientists had been denied grants for research support by the National Institutes of Health because of a question of their "loyalty." Press coverage of the meetings and a request from the academy for information from the Department of Health, Education, and Welfare generated sufficient interest in the matter that a statement by the secretary of the department was issued describing HEW's policies in connection with the award of research grants. The secretary's statement indicated that since June of 1952 the department, although it did not require security or loyalty investigations for recipients of research grants, did in fact deny support to scientists when information of a substantial nature brought to the attention of the department satisfied it that the individual was engaging in or had engaged in subversive activities or that there was a serious question of his loyalty to the United States.

The HEW policy created a dilemma for the foundation, especially if it were to proceed with making grants to individuals who had been denied grants from HEW because of doubted loyalty. Senior staff discussions within the foundation, initiated by the director in anticipation of inquiries regarding NSF policies in this area, led to a position that the foundation should not make security checks on its prospective grantees, because its support was for unclassified research and because, inasmuch as the grant went to the recipient's institution, the institution was fundamentally responsible for its faculty or staff. Thus, the only consideration in the award of basic research grants by NSF would continue to be the investigator's competence and the importance of the problem.

Endorsed by the foundation's Divisional Committee on Biological and Medical Sciences and by the National Science Board at its meeting in May of 1954, the policy, in essence, stated:

> In appraising a proposal submitted by or on behalf of a scientist for the support of unclassified research not involving considerations of security, the Foundation will be guided as to an individual's experience, competence, and integrity by the judgment of scientists having a working knowledge of his qualifications.[27]

Discussion within the National Science Board established limiting conditions for the policy: The foundation would not knowingly support the research of an avowed Communist or an individual who had been determined to be a Communist by judicial proceedings or by an unappealed determination of the attorney general or the Subversive Activities Control Board, or of an individual who advocated change in the form of government by other than constitutional means. Persons convicted of sabotage would also be excluded from NSF support. The policy was endorsed by the American Association for the Advancement of Science at its annual meeting in 1954. Subsequently in 1956, the National Academy of Sciences, following a request for review from the White House, supported the foundation's position. At this point President Eisenhower directed all federal government agencies to adopt the policy.

As Philip Smith points out, in this particular issue the foundation influenced governmentwide policy through its own de-

27. *National Science Foundation Sixth Annual Report, 1956,* NSF-57-1 (Washington, D.C.: U.S. Government Printing Office, 1956), 9.

liberations and adoption of a position with respect to academic science support. The adopted policy changed the nature of the debate from "guilty unless affirming loyalty" to "if scientifically acceptable, loyal unless proven unloyal."[28] For those who did not experience the McCarthy period, the political courage inherent in the foundation's action at this stage of its development may be difficult to comprehend. That it was taken in the face of opposition from a cabinet-level department, in the absence of any support from the executive office of the president, and against a formidable senatorial presence who had yet to be confronted by his colleagues, adds to the foundation's stature. The action would serve to remind a subsequent National Science Board during a period of difficulty in the 1960s, of appropriate standards to be upheld regarding the support of controversial individuals.

The closing years of the 1950s and early years of the 1960s represent a high-water mark of science policy efforts within the executive branch of government. In the executive office of the president, stimulated largely by the effects of Sputnik, a number of actions were taken to significantly change both the responsibility and the procedures for generating science policy, including academic science policy.

The most important of these actions was made as a part of Reorganization Plan No. 2 of 1962, which established the Office of Science and Technology.[29] Much of the foundation's responsibility for science policy was reassigned to this newly created Office. The president's message forwarding the plan to Congress stated:

> The Foundation will continue to originate policy proposals and recommendations concerning the support of basic research and education in the sciences, and the new Office will look to the Foundation to provide stud-

28. Smith, *The National Science Board,* 19.
29. Reorganization Plan No. 2 of 1962, submitted to Congress by President Kennedy on 29 March, 1962. (The Reorganization Act of 1949 authorizes reorganization within the executive branch of the federal government through plans submitted by the chief executive to the Congress which are effective unless acted upon negatively by the Congress within sixty days after the date of submission.)

ies and information on which sound national policies in science and technology can be based.

In addition to the Office of Science and Technology, the organizational structure within the executive office would now consist of the Federal Council for Science and Technology (representing government agencies concerned with research and development) and the President's Science Advisory Committee, which advised the government on all possible problems in research and development. The overall enterprise was under the guidance and direction of the same individual, who also served as personal advisor to the president.

How the National Science Foundation functioned within this structure is indicated by Smith as follows:

> In this period, the NSF, largely through the Director, and to some extent, the NSB Chairman and Board Members, was a regular participant in the triad of activities centered in the Executive Office. . . . After Sputnik, the NSF budget grew enormously [and] the Director and the Board [gave] their principal attention to the NSF's expanding programs.[30]

This was the denouement of the Budget Bureau's effort to have the foundation develop either for itself or for the federal government as a whole some form of all-inclusive science policy. The director of the foundation, opposed to the idea from the beginning, summed up his view of the issue and answered critics of the foundation in his resumé of the foundation's first decade:

> Those who insist that policy must be handed down "ready made" in the form of a proclamation or edict do not understand the nature of policy in the realm of science. To be workable, policy must evolve on the basis of experience; further, it must take fully into account

30. Smith, *The National Science Board,* 9. In the post-Sputnik era, NSF appropriations increased as follows: fiscal year 1960, $154.8 million; fiscal year 1965, $420.4 million; fiscal year 1970, $438.0 million; fiscal year 1975, $763.3 million; fiscal year 1980, $903.8 million; fiscal year 1983, $1.092 billion.

the fundamental principles essential to the effective performance of research in science.[31]

Years of Transition and Transformation

In the ten-year span between fiscal years 1954 and 1964,
federal government research and development expenditures
grew from slightly over 3 billion to 14.7 billion dollars.[32] This
growth gave rise to a series of congressional hearings, the first
of which was initiated in 1963 by a select committee headed
by Congressman Carl Elliott.[33] The establishment of the Elliott
Committee was quickly followed by the appointment of a second special committee, under the chairmanship of Congressman Emilio Q. Daddario.[34] Both groups were given broad terms
of reference: They were to review the scientific research and
development programs supported by all agencies of the federal
government. With particular reference to academic science policy, the critical issue was the institutional (frequently referred
to euphemistically as "geographic") distribution of funds for
academic science.

The foundation, along with other science supporting agencies, was asked to comment on the question

Is it possible to achieve greater uniformity in the geographic distribution of Federal contracts and grants

31. Alan T. Waterman, "National Science Foundation: A Ten Year Resumé."
Science, 6 May 1960, 1341–54.

32. *Federal Funds for Research, Development and Other Activities,* vol. 18,
NSF-69-31 (Washington, D.C.: U.S. Government Printing Office, 1969).

33. H.R. 504, 88th Congress, 1st sess. 11 September 1963. The select committee (Elliott Committee) created by this resolution issued ten reports based
on its hearings, the first being dated 10 August 1964, and the last 18 February
1965. They are available from the U.S. Government Printing Office, Washington, D.C.

34. Subcommittee on Science, Research, and Development, House Committee on Science and Astronautics, *A Statement of Purpose,* Report no. 1,
88th Congress, 1st sess., December 1963. The Daddario Committee issued a
series of five reports based on this series of hearings and special subcommittee
studies, the last dated December 1964. They are available from the U.S. Government Printing Office, Washington, D.C.

without affecting the quality or cost of research and development?

The response to that question by the foundation was

Unequivocally "no." Briefly, to achieve high quality results requires going where the best capability exists. That capability is now quite concentrated geographically. Hence the maintenance of high quality results will result in concentration unless and until we build up a broader geographic base of capability. And this will require additional expenditures.

This does not mean that we are helpless in the effort to assure more widespread distribution of support for research and development. What it does mean is that we cannot hope to obtain maximum output of research and development results unless we support and use the facilities and the scientists and engineers in our great centers of scientific and technological activity. Hence if we are interested in research of high quality, done with minimum delay, we must not go to the institutions which would first have to build up a capability and then begin to accomplish the job that we want done.[35]

On the basis of testimony at their hearings, both committees reported findings which supported the contention that federal research funds were concentrated in a comparatively small number of institutions. In the words of the Daddario Committee, the problem was "severe enough, the needs and potential benefits involved are great enough, to warrant continued attention by Congress and the Executive Branch."[36]

The issue of institutional distribution of research funds was brought to a head by President Johnson in September 1965, through a presidential directive:

The strength of the research and developmental programs of the major agencies, and hence their ability to

35. Subcommittee on Science, Research and Development, House Committee on Science and Astronautics, *Geographic Distribution of Federal Research and Development Funds,* Government and Science Report no. 4, 88th Congress, 2d sess., 1964.
36. Ibid., 48.

meet national needs, depends heavily upon the total strength of our university system. Research supported to further agency missions should be administered not only with a view to producing specific results, but also with a view to strengthening academic institutions and increasing the number of institutions capable of performing research of high quality.[37]

To understand the full import of the president's statement on academic science policy, it must be viewed in the context of a much broader educational policy statement which had been enunciated previously. In his Education Program Message, the president had asked Congress to support the goal of "an educational system restudied, reinforced, and revitalized." With specific reference to higher education, there was a request for programs "to help small and less well developed colleges improve their programs."[38] President Johnson's academic science policy statement of September 1965 thus augmented his more general policies relating to support for higher education per se.

In response to the president's directive, executive branch agencies broadened the scope of academic science support. The National Science Foundation expanded its University Science Development Program and, in addition, initiated the Departmental Science Development and the College Science Improvement programs. The Department of Defense launched Project Themis, aimed at academic institutions not then heavily engaged in federallly sponsored research. The National Institutes of Health supplemented their institutional grants with a developmental program, the Health Sciences Advancement Award.

Following extensive testimony on the performance of the National Science Foundation since its establishment, the Daddario subcommittee issued a report on its findings.[39] On 16

37. Memorandum from President Lyndon B. Johnson to Heads of Departments and Agencies, "Strengthening Academic Capabilities for Science throughout the Country," 13 September 1965.

38. Message from the President of the United States Transmitting the Education Program, 12 January 1965.

39. Report of the House Committee on Science and Astronautics, *The National Science Foundation: Its Present and Future*, 89th Congress, 2d sess., 1966.

March 1966, The first version of what would become known popularly as the Daddario bill (H.R. 13696) was introduced in the House. Intended in its first form to stimulate discussion and to elicit opinions from a wide audience, the bill went through several versions before being passed by the House and forwarded to the Senate. In the Senate, a companion bill was introduced by Senator Edward Kennedy in October 1967 (S. 2598). After Senate hearings and passage, the Daddario-Kennedy Amendment emerged from conference and was signed into law by President Johnson on 8 July 1968.[40]

The Daddario-Kennedy Amendment significantly changed the National Science Foundation in both form and substance. Of particular importance for higher education, the amendment designated the social sciences as a field eligible for foundation support. Also of importance for academic science, it established a legislative basis for the board and the director to recommend and pursue national policies for basic research and education in the sciences. Among its other features, the amendment authorized the foundation to support applied as well as basic research, it broadened National Science Foundation authority in international science activities, and it required the National Science Board to report annually to the Congress, through the president, on the state of science in the United States. The new legislation also provided for annual hearings before both House and Senate science committees to review the foundation's programs and to authorize appropriation levels for the following fiscal year. (Under the legislation which had governed it previously, the foundation was required to appear only before the respective appropriations subcommittees of the House and Senate.) The Daddario-Kennedy Amendment also made a number of important organizational changes within the foundation, the most important of these being to remove from "career status" to "political status" five senior staff positions, establishing the requirement that the deputy director and four assistant directors, in addition to the director, be ap-

40. NSF Act of 1950 as amended, P.L. 90-407, 90th Congress, 2d sess., 18 July 1968.

pointed by the president, by and with the advice and consent of the Senate.

Although the research support programs and policies of the foundation had not completely eschewed applied science prior to the Daddario-Kennedy legislation, its passage did confront the foundation with an explicit responsibility to respond to its new authority. As in any attempt to initiate new program activities, there were a number of problems.

Program development under the newly acquired authority was carried out under somewhat less than auspicious conditions. The term of the foundation's second director, Leland J. Haworth, was approaching its last year. The election of Richard M. Nixon as president meant not only that there would be in all probability a new director for NSF, but that the foundation would have to adapt to a new administration whose attitudes toward science were not entirely friendly. A state of apprehension throughout the science agencies of the government and among academic scientists led the publisher of *Science,* Dr. Dael Wolfle, to address an open letter to President Nixon in which he stated: "The substantial amount of uncertainty that exists concerning future plans and future funding levels for research and other scientific activities suggests that it would be useful to have an authoritative statement of the science policies of the federal government."[41]

The foundation's first response in defining its conception of applied science support comprised an interdisciplinary approach in a number of selected areas. These included research on solar and geothermal energy, water management, earthquake hazards and their mitigation, and studies of particular policy issues such as land use and the impact of federal regulations on various private sector activities. This proposed program was titled "Interdisciplinary Research Relevant to Problems of our Society" (IRRPOS), and was the product of a task force within the NSF staff drawn largely from engineering and the social sciences. At the foundation's authorization hearings for the fiscal year 1970 budget, the proposed program was not warmly received. Congressman Daddario,

41. "Open letter to the Honorable, The President of the United States, from Dr. Dael Wolfle, Publisher," *Science,* 12 December 1969.

particularly, felt that the foundation had not "thought through" its approach to the new program area and was still "groping" for appropriate support concepts. Consequently the request for 1970 IRRPOS funds was sharply reduced.

Meanwhile, the process of finding a new director for the foundation was underway. In the course of this activity, the name of Dr. Frank Long, a chemist from Cornell University, had been presented to the White House by the National Science Board. But it turned out that Dr. Long had publicly expressed differences with President Nixon regarding a proposed anti-ballistic missile system. Following a series of unsuccessful attempts to make some accommodation in the situation, Dr. Long withdrew from consideration as a candidate and Dr. William McElroy, an experimental biologist from Johns Hopkins University, was appointed the foundation's third director.

Dr. McElroy made it known from the beginning that he intended the administration of the foundation to be different under his leadership than it had been under that of his predecessors. Very early he announced a goal of increasing the foundation's appropriation to $1 billion within three years from its then $400 million level. Regarding the foundation's policy role, at a series of hearings on technology assessment held by the Subcommittee on Science, Research, and Development of the House Committee on Science and Astronautics, he stated the intention of the foundation to be active in policy-recommending activities which,

> although not necessarily scientific in themselves, require an appreciation of the scientific factor. . . . The Foundation must further develop reasoned positions on such fundamental matters as the magnitude and distribution of the scientific research component of the Federal budget, needs for research in specific fields, opportunities for exploiting scientific events and developments in the national interest, and the means for meeting the needs for specialized scientific and technical manpower.[42]

42. Testimony of William D. McElroy, Director, National Science Foundation, *Hearings on Technology Assessment before the Subcommittee on Science, Research and Development, House Committee on Science and Astronautics,* 91st Congress, 1st sess., 18 November 1969.

Dr. McElroy stated that the essence of the administration's view of science would be that "science must serve society and society must serve science." Translated, Dr. McElroy explained, this becomes a question of "effective relevance—how the concerns of science and society can be made more relevant to each other."[43] The approach, as described, would bring together scientists from different disciplines and merge them into teams for the study of national problems—for example, energy and water needs, genetic effects of chemical additives, and pollution of air and water. These studies would draw upon the resources of the national laboratories at Oak Ridge, Brookhaven, and Argonne, as well as upon the academic scientific community.

The new director's approach to IRRPOS was to place it under the administrative responsibility of a newly created Office of Interdisciplinary Research and to push hard, not only for obligation of the program's initial appropriation, but for an improved presentation of the program within the budget for fiscal year 1971. The program survived the hearings on the 1971 budget and in its fiscal 1972 request, the foundation asked for funds at the same level as the previous year. But, as the budget progressed through the Bureau of the Budget (which had been reorganized by President Nixon and renamed the Office of Management and Budget), IRRPOS changed from a modest effort into a major foundation program to be known as Research Applied to National Needs (RANN).

This dramatic change stemmed from a shift in government spending policy that President Nixon had initiated in the interest of stimulating the sagging economy. The president had directed the Office of Management and Budget (OMB) to find ways to increase spending by federal agencies during the 1972 budgetary year. The Office of Management and Budget was quick to take advantage of this policy directive to influence what it had for some time viewed as a badly needed shift in the direction of NSF programs. In exchange for added funds in the amount of some $100 million for the total NSF budget

43. Speech to the American Institute of Physics, as reported by the *New York Times,* 6 October 1970, 1. See also *Science,* 4 October 1970, 144–46.

in fiscal year 1972 (a portion of which would be applied to RANN) the OMB proposed that the foundation terminate its institutional support programs. In addition, the foundation was to modify the science education efforts by eliminating teacher institute programs and by shifting other education activities away from aid to higher quality students and toward the upgrading of science activities of small colleges, especially those attended by black students. Last, some of the added funds were to be used to pick up projects no longer eligible for support by the Department of Defense because of the so-called Mansfield Amendment, which had made it unlawful for the department to finance basic research that was not directly related to military needs or operations. As a sort of reward for this, the foundation would be allowed to ask Congress for increased research support funds. Among the conditions attached to the proposal was that the applied research effort would be restructured and removed from the administration of the research divisions. It was to be placed under the supervision of a newly created unit which would aggressively seek potential grantees instead of waiting to receive research proposals—a traditional characteristic of the basic research supporting programs.

The negotiations that led to the decisions and the consequent program policies and arrangements that established RANN were carried out directly between the staff of the Office of Management and Budget and the director and certain senior staff of the foundation. The OMB was utilizing an opportunity offered by prevailing White House economic policy to shape the policy and program direction of the foundation, and the event introduced a marked change in the traditional mode of internal interaction between the director and the National Science Board with reference to program development and the establishment of policies that would guide the foundation.

When subsequently presented by the director to the board for its "approval," the newly defined RANN program had proceeded so far in redefinition and restructuring and had so much higher administration force behind it that in all respects it was a fait accompli. The board's approval was, in fact, less important than were the actions that had finessed the role of the board in policy formulation and had altered traditional director-board relationships. Under the foundation's first two directors, there had been close and constant cooperation, marked by successful prevention of intrusion by the Bureau of the Budget into the foundation's internal organization and policy formulation. Under the administration of the foundation's third director, there was a significant diminution of cooperation and a consequent diminished role of the board in controlling foundation policies. The Office of Management and Budget essentially became the foundation's "protector" from that point on, and policy was determined largely through budget decisions. As we shall later see, the tendencies established by OMB decision making that established RANN would come into full flower in the 1980s.

The decade of the 1970s was an unsettled period for the foundation. No little part of this condition was caused by the rapid turnover in the office of the director. Two and one-half years into his six-year term, Director McElroy left the foundation to accept the chancellorship of the University of California at San Diego. Between February 1972 and November 1982, the foundation experienced the leadership of three directors: Dr. H. Guyford Stever, who served four years; Dr. Richard Atkinson, who served four years; and Dr. John Slaughter, who served two years. Of these three administrations, Dr. Stever's was marked by the fact that he served, for a portion of his term, as science advisor to President Nixon following the abolition of the Office of Science and Technology in January of 1973.[44]

Foundation research programs during this period were marked by an active thrust toward linkage of the newly instituted applied research effort with industrial enterprises. Basic research

44. In November 1982, President Reagan appointed Dr. Edward A. Knapp, a physicist from Los Alamos Laboratory, director of the foundation. The instability in the executive direction of the foundation which started during the 1970s was exacerbated by the fact that within the first month of his tenure, Director Knapp "accepted" the resignations of the deputy director and three assistant directors, all of whom had been appointed in the Carter administration. The implicit politicization of the foundation, inherent in the Daddario-Kennedy Amendment, thus became explicit.

activities continued in traditional ways and, as we shall later note, prospered during the administration of President Carter after losing some ground to short-range applied science. There was less enthusiasm both in the executive office of the president and in the foundation for science education programs, although congressional interest remained strong. In general, there was a marked shift toward broadening the mission in these programs to increase access of previously ignored constituencies, including women, the physically handicapped, and ethnic minority groups. Thus, in keeping with social and political trends, "equal opportunity" attenuated excellence to a significant degree in the foundation's science education effort.

Congressional critics of foundation programs were vocal during the 1970s. Senator William Proxmire, particularly, used the foundation as a whipping boy with his monthly "Golden Fleece" awards for projects he considered wasteful of federal funds. The social sciences experienced a resurgence of congressional displeasure. This time it came in the form of criticism of a precollege curriculum reform effort in social science entitled "Man—A Course of Study," popularly referred to as Project MACOS. Congressman John Conlan of Arizona charged that the products of this project somehow distorted basic family values. One result of this imbroglio was an attempt on the part of the House to require that all projects supported by the foundation await final approval by the Congress before they could be funded. Fortunately, wiser congressional heads prevailed, although the threatened action indicated the estate to which academic science support programs had fallen in the legislative branch of the federal government.

At the time of the congressional hearings on the Daddario-Kennedy legislation, as well as in subsequent hearings held in 1970, the role of the National Science Foundation in policy formulation and the relationship of the board to the Office of Science and Technology and the President's Science Advisory Committee were discussed at length. Of particular concern to the subcommittee was the extent to which the board was independent of the two executive agents.

Dr. Philip Handler, president of the National Academy of Sciences, pointed out that the President's Science Advisory Committee was brought into being to provide the president with competent advice on problems which are scientific, technological, and managerial in character. The policy considerations facing the President's Advisory Committee were thus concerned with the application of science or the development of new technology rather than with the growth of science per se. Despite a history of hesitation in assuming a policy role, Dr. Handler felt that the experience of the National Science Board with the development of programs within the foundation, plus the board's mixed composition of working scientists, academic administrators, and industrial scientific directors, rendered it a most appropriate body to develop broad policy for science and science education. Dr. Handler summarized his argument as follows:

> This, then, is the pattern I foresee for the next several years: PSAC-OST will be largely concerned with policy and technological problems related to specific agency and interagency missions affecting all phases of American life while NSB-NSF will be mainly concerned with the progress of science and science education including the problems of scientific manpower, science information, provision of research resources and the welfare and development of the institutions in which science and science education are conducted. Both bodies will continue to see means by which science and technology may improve the human condition, but these opportunities are so diverse, unlimited, and challenging that we can only hope that this combination will prove equal to the total task.[45]

Mr. Eric Walker, a former chairman of the National Science Board and past president of the National Academy of Engineering, took a much dimmer view of the possibility of an effective role in policy matters for the board. He was particularly distressed by what he perceived as a gradual and sys-

45. Philip Handler, "Federal Science Policy," *Science,* 3 March 1967, 1066.

tematic deterioration of the board's role in policymaking. This deterioration had progressed to such a point that he felt it "not strange, therefore, that the board has been regarded in some quarters as an ineffective body, nor that it has been charged with neglecting some of its basic duties." He was apprehensive that unless there were provisions to "strengthen the National Science Board, we are likely to witness a gradual shift of the control of National Science policies (including academic science policy) . . . from the scientific community to the bureaucracy."[46]

Throughout the hearings, there was a recurrent expression of uncertainty on the part of witnesses regarding federal government policies toward science, especially academic science. The uncertainty was due, according to Dr. Handler, "to a concatenation of circumstances" resulting in a situation in which "morale of the scientific community is lower than at any time since the Second World War." Dr. H. E. Carter, chairman of the National Science Board and provost of the University of Illinois, addressed his testimony specifically to "government-science-education relationships."[47]

Dr. Carter's reference to "government-science-education" relationships recognized the fact that a transition in federal government relationships with higher education, initiated by Sputnik in 1957, had taken place. The first legislative expression of that change was the National Defense Education Act of 1958, which was followed by an even stronger and less doubtful expression in the Higher Education Act of 1965. During the transition, questions of academic science policy had been caught up in general higher education issues. Insofar as the National Science Foundation was concerned, the Daddario-Kennedy Amendment had changed the foundation's character from that of an agency associated almost exclusively with science as a function of higher education to an agency that in-

46. Eric A. Walker, "National Science Board," *Science,* 28 April 1967, 477.
47. Report of the Subcommittee on Science, Research and Development to the Committee on Science and Astronautics, 91st Congress, *Towards a Science Policy for the United States* (Washington, D.C.: U.S Government Printing Office, 1970).

creasingly connected science and its applications to technology. By the late 1970s, the programs of the foundation reflected values that were an unstable mixture of Bush's and Kilgore's conceptions. It was no longer exclusively the patron of basic research and science education, but was equally concerned with science as it related to problems of the society sponsoring it. Whatever uniqueness had marked the National Science Foundation's relationships with the higher education community during its first eighteen years no longer existed but was being shared by other programs that had moved on stage following Sputnik and the Daddario-Kennedy Amendment to the National Science Foundation Act of 1950.

2

Higher Education Per Se

The National Defense Education Act and
"Better Things to Come"

On the occasion of the tenth anniversary of the National Defense Education Act (September 1968) President Lyndon B. Johnson recalled with obvious pride, the enactment of that legislation:

> Ten years and 1 month ago, I made a speech to my Senate colleagues about a bill we were acting upon.
>
> "History may well record," I told them, "that we saved liberty and saved freedom when we undertook a crash program in the field of education . . . I hope this bill is only the forerunner of better things to come."
>
> Today, as we celebrate the 10th anniversary of the law, we may not yet be able to prove that NDEA saved liberty—but surely it has enriched and strengthened the freedom we enjoy. And surely that bill—the first large-scale modern program of Federal aid to education—has proven to be the forerunner of better things to come.[1]

While recognizing the "dollars and books" aspect of NDEA, it was President Johnson's belief that the historical importance of this legislation lay in the fact that it paved the way for a

---

1. President's speech to the fiftieth annual convention of the American Legion, White House Press Office, 10 September 1968, New Orleans, La. (Reference: National Defense Education Act of 1958. (P.L. 85-864).

"new era of support for education in America" and that it served as a "symbol of our Nation's most important purpose: to fulfill the individual—his freedom, his happiness, his promise." Regarding the fundamental constitutional question as to whether the federal government has a role in the affairs of education, President Johnson replied, "The answer this law gave was a loud 'Yes.' "

The issue of the federal role in the affairs of higher education, brought to a head dramatically by the events surrounding the Soviet launching of Sputnik, had been on the horizon of the national political agenda for some time. Starting with President Hoover's National Advisory Committee on Education in 1931,[2] presidential advisory groups had repeatedly pointed out the need and desirability of resolving the inconsistent and frequently conflicting policies of federal agencies in their interactions with the higher education community. But such recommendations met with unenthusiastic reception within the leadership of higher education. Generally speaking, university presidents took the position that it was better to live with a highly disorganized federal "system" than to take the risk of potential interference and perhaps reduced availability of funds that a more-coordinated and better-managed government effort might bring. As Homer Babbidge pointed out, the "economic royalists" of higher education did well under conditions of organizational deficiency in government programs and they were quick to use the cover of "academic freedom" in opposing a more systematized effort that would allow the less-favored institutions to fare somewhat better.[3]

Over and above such parochial interests, there were strong cultural and social forces that historically had impeded the development of effective federal policies for support of education at all levels, including higher education. Although World War II had been an effective agent in bringing academic science

2. For a summary of policy recommendations by presidential commissions, see Chester E. Finn, Jr., *Scholars, Dollars, and Bureaucrats* (Washington, D.C.: Brookings Institution, 1978), chap. 7.

3. Homer D. Babbidge, "Scientists Affluent, Humanists Militant: Faction in Higher Education," *Graduate Journal Supplement* (University of Texas, Austin, Texas) 5 (1962): 162.

onto the national agenda and initiating federal government programs for its support as a continuing peacetime function, higher education per se confronted issues that were only tangential to academic science. Among the more important ones were the lack of constitutional authority, the widespread fear of federal government control of education, the church-state issue and the problem of support for church-related institutions, and the racial issue represented by segregated educational institutions.

The emergence of higher education as a "policy arena" is noted by Wolanin and Gladieux as taking place in the late 1950s and the early 1960s.[4] Within the Congress, institutional definition was enhanced in 1957 with the creation of the Subcommittee on Education within the House Education and Labor Committee. Shortly thereafter, President Eisenhower responded to the confrontation of Sputnik with recommendations for an expanded National Science Foundation and for a number of new education programs which eventually were authorized by Congress in the National Defense Education Act of 1958. Although these education programs initiated by NDEA were heavily slanted in the direction of improving science education and were presented as temporary emergency measures to counter the Soviet achievements in scientific manpower training and research, this was landmark legislation.

In the context of federal policy for the support of higher education, the National Defense Education Act had three notable features.[5] Of primary importance was the fact that the

4. T. R. Wolanin and L. E. Gladieux, "The Political Culture of a Policy Arena: Higher Education," in *What Government Does,* ed. M. Holden and D. L. Dresang (New York: Sage, 1975).

5. The National Defense Education Act was the first of what came to be referred to as "omnibus bills" encompassing a variety of loosely related education programs. The legislation, as passed, covered some ten areas of support, including those within elementary and secondary education. Of primary interest to higher education were programs involving loans to college students (with partial forgiveness if the student later taught in secondary or elementary school); fellowships for graduate students; and financial assistance for strengthening instruction in science, mathematics, modern foreign languages, and "other critical subjects."

As compared to the open-ended language of the National Science Foun-

principal benefits were directed towards students rather than institutions. Never before had Congress enunciated the national policy that "no student of ability will be denied the opportunity for higher education because of financial need."

Second was the distributive nature of fellowships and the institutional benefits of NDEA. In this respect the legislation followed populist rather than the competitive elitist policies that were reflected in the National Science Foundation Act and its programs, which had resulted in the concentration of funds in a few, research-oriented institutions.

Third was a loyalty oath and an affidavit disclaiming membership or belief in the aims of subversive organizations.[6] Both had to be executed by individuals who were prospective beneficiaries of NDEA programs. Section 1001 (f) of the act stated that:

> No part of any funds appropriated or otherwise made available . . . shall be used to make payment or loans to any individual unless such individual (1) has executed and filed with the Commissioner an affidavit that he does not believe in and is not a member of and does not support any organization that believes in or teaches the overthrow of the United States Government by force or violence or by any illegal or unconstitutional methods, and (2) has taken or submitted to an oath or affidavit in the following form: "I do solemnly swear or affirm that I will bear true faith and allegiance to the United States of America and will support and defend the constitution and laws of the United States against all its enemies, foreign and domestic. . . .

Reaction to the oath and affidavit requirement was widespread within civil rights and education associations, and par-

dation Act of 1950, NDEA and subsequent education legislation defined administrative policies rather explicitly. Instructions to the commissioner of education and, not infrequently, to the secretary of health, education, and welfare left little room for the exercise of imagination in program development and administration.

6. An especially cogent discussion of the oath and affidavit issue in NDEA is included in H. R. Babbidge and R. M. Rosenzweig, *The Federal Interest in Higher Education* (New York: McGraw-Hill, 1962), 158ff.

ticularly within the higher education community. Congressional debate, especially in the Senate, accompanied by actions of a significant number of the nation's leading colleges and universities that opted not to participate in NDEA under conditions that required the oath and affidavit, led in 1961 to an NDEA amendment dropping the affidavit but retaining the oath. The amendment also clarified the law by making it a crime for an individual belonging to a subversive group to receive funds under NDEA programs.

The experience of the oath and affidavit turmoil created by the NDEA legislation lends credence to the arguments of those who believe that it is impossible to enjoy the benefits of federal government support without simultaneously risking the intrusion of government into the affairs of colleges and universities. And the argument is weakened only slightly by recalling that however nefarious the behavior of the Congress in this respect, the hysteria over communism and national security was shared in varying degrees by every major institutional component of our society during the period. But, as pointed out by Babbidge and Rosenzweig, the more important lesson to be learned is that there is vitality enough in our political and educational systems, if it is exercised in timely fashion, either to prevent the imposition of repugnant conditions within government support programs or to gain recourse from such impositions when and if they do occur.

With the passage of the National Defense Education Act, the question of federal government support for higher education per se was resolved in the affirmative, albeit with qualifications. From that point on, in the matrix of relationships between the federal government and higher education, the academic science programs would slowly be forced from center stage and overshadowed by more-direct higher education support policies and programs. The GI Bill (1944) had been instrumental in generating an unprecedented flow of students into the colleges and universities. The decade following NDEA would see a stream of legislation that would expand and redefine relationships between the federal government and the higher education community.

In March 1961, President John Kennedy sent a special message on education to Congress which stated:

> Our twin goals must be: a new standard of excellence in education—and the availability of such excellence to all who are willing and able to pursue it.

In two subsequent messages on education, he recommended extension of the college-housing loan program and, in addition to existing loan programs, a scholarship program for talented and needy students, including as a component, cost of education payments to the institutions attended.[7] In its final form, the higher education bill in the Eighty-seventh Congress (1962) provided: (1) Physical plant construction aid in the form of grants and loans, with grant funds being limited to science, engineering, and library buildings; (2) a student loan program, with a portion of the loans to be "nonreimbursable"; and (3) grants to states for construction of community colleges, limited to science, engineering, and library buildings. House floor action recommited the bill with instruction to strike the student loan program, and the bill died in conference.

In 1963, a new omnibus education bill was sent to the Congress which, in its higher education components, provided for federal assistance for academic facility construction, a greatly expanded NDEA loan and fellowship effort, student aid in the form of insured loans, work-study, and scholarships for both talented and needy students, and assistance for college libraries.[8] Congress, in considering the new legislation, essentially started from the points of agreement in its effort to pass legislation the year before. Largely ignoring the scholarship and student aid recommendations, legislation came out of the Congress as the Higher Education Facilities Act of 1963 (P.L. 88-204). It was signed into law in December 1963 by President Lyndon Johnson following his accession to the presidency after the assassination of President Kennedy.

7. President Kennedy sent three special messages on education to the Congress: 20 February 1961, 6 February 1962, and 29 January 1963.
8. National Education Improvement Act of 1963, 29 January 1963.

The years of President Johnson's administrations are frequently referred to by college and university administrators as the "golden years" for higher education in the post–World War II period. Certainly at no time before and at no time since has education, both higher and lower-school education, been as high on the national agenda of any administration. On 1 November 1964, a policy paper on education was issued by the White House which indicated President Johnson's fundamental view on education:

> I believe every child has the right to as much education as he has the ability to receive. I believe this right does not end in the lower schools, but goes on through technical and higher education—if the child wants it and can use it.

The president went on to outline a program of action, pledging that he would "put education at the head of our work agenda," and by concentrating the effort in combination with "our war on poverty" break "the chains of ignorance" for "those who are poverty's prisoners." This theme would be reiterated in a number of special messages to the Congress during the Johnson years[9]—years which would see the passage of legislation to provide for the construction of classrooms, libraries, and dormitories; increase the number of scholarships, fellowships, and loans for students; provide funds for "developing" institutions; initiate work-study programs; and establish the National Endowment on the Arts and the Humanities (1965), to do for the arts and humanities what the National Science Foundation had been doing for the sciences. Perhaps of greater significance than the breadth of these legislative enactments was the fact that with the passage of the Higher Education Facilities Act in 1963, the "national defense" overtones which inhered in NDEA were displaced by an emerging appreciation of the value of supporting higher education for its own sake.

With the passage of the Higher Education Act of 1965 (P.L. 89-329), the basic legislative charter for a continuing relation-

9. President Johnson sent three special messages on education to the Congress: 12 January 1965, 1 March 1966, 28 February 1967.

ship between the federal government and higher education was established. In contrast to the "defense," emergency, and other limiting characteristics of NDEA legislation, the Higher Education Act was distinguished by its scope, its financial commitment, and by its broad and clear definition of purpose. Among other things, the act authorized almost a billon dollars for its first year of operations; included the first program of undergraduate scholarships; created a new program of federally guaranteed and subsidized student loans and an expanded work-study program; and initiated programs for community service and continuing education, library assistance, training and research, strengthening developing institutions, teacher training, improvement of undergraduate instruction, and expansion of support for facilities construction.

The Higher Education Act of 1965 marked "the coming of age of education policy as an aspect of national social policy."[10] Although there would be future elaborations and modifications, the next substantive step in higher education policy would not come until 1972, when the concept of institutional aid would be rejected by the Congress in favor of student assistance as the preferred mode of federal support.

While there are exceptions, leaders in higher education would generally agree with President Johnson's tenth anniversary assertion that NDEA did indeed pave the way for a "new era of support" for higher education in the United States.[11] Whether

10. The "coming of age" of any policy is a complex development and higher education policy was no exception. An idea, from the time of its inception until it sees the light of day in legislaton, will be discussed, debated, formulated, and revised through various steps in the political process. For discussions of the 1972 amendments to the Higher Education Act of 1965 that give excellent insights into this process, see L. E. Gladieux and T. R. Wolanin, *Congress and the Colleges* (Lexington, Mass.: D. C. Heath, 1976), and C. E. Finn, Jr., *Education and the Presidency* (Lexington, Mass.: D. C. Heath, 1977). The quotation is from the Foreword (p. x) to Finn, written by Senator Daniel P. Moynihan.

11. Differences of opinion regarding government support for higher education may be based upon principle and/or upon assessment of results. A classic statement against government support of higher education, based primarily on principle, is: John A. Howard, "Principles in Default" (Speech delivered at the annual meeting of American Association of Presidents of Independent Colleges and Universities, French Lick, Indiana, 6 December 1974). See also

his hope that NDEA had "saved liberty and saved freedom" and that it would prove to be "the forerunner of better things to come" is more problematic. There were those who thought that its passage presaged just the opposite. Senator Goldwater prophesied, "If adopted, the legislation will mark the inception of aid, supervision, and ultimately control of education in this country by Federal authorities."[12] And perhaps more important but less obvious, the enforcement of social legislation enacted in the mid-1960s simultaneously with much of the higher education legislation carried with it implications analogous to the oath and affadivit encroachment on academic freedoms inherent in traditional customs and practices of colleges and universities.

Sturm und Drang: The Nixon Period

The closing years of President Johnson's administration and the years encompassing the administration of President Nixon marked a period of *Sturm und Drang* for higher education. Continuing widespread campus disorders which had started in the mid-1960s stimulated hearings in both houses of Congress. Various authorization and appropriation acts carried provisions for cutting off federal funds for students and faculty convicted of crimes connected with disruptive campus activities.

The pertinent language of the Higher Education Amendments Act of 1968 (P.L. 90-575), 16 October 1968, which served as a prototype for other bills, states:

Section 504. (a) If an institution of higher education determines, after affording notice and opportunity for

R. A. Freeman, "Federal Aid, No!—Facts, Figures and a Primrose Path" *Graduate Journal Supplement* (University of Texas, Austin, Texas) 5 (1962): 29–39. The case for federal government support of higher education is persuasively made in the same journal: Publius, "Listen to the People," 9–25. (Publius in this instance is Cynthia Huxall Gardner, editor of the 1962 *Supplement* issue.)

12. "Minority views of Senators Barry Goldwater and John G. Tower," *National Defense Education Amendments of 1961*, S. report 652, 87, no. 1: 117.

hearing to an individual attending or employed by, such institution, that such individual has been convicted, by any court of record of any crime which was committed after the date of enactment of this Act and which involved the use of (or assistance to others in the use of) force, disruption, or the seizure of property under control of any institution of higher education to prevent officials or students in such institution from engaging in their duties or pursuing their studies, and that such crime was of a serious nature and contributed to a substantial disruption of the administration of the institution with respect to which such crime was committed, then the institution which such individual attends, or is employed by, shall deny for a period of two years any further payment to, or for the direct benefit of, such individual under any of the programs specified in subsection (c). If an institution denies an individual assistance under the authority of the preceding sentence of this subsection, then any institution which such individual subsequently attends shall deny for the remainder of the two-year period any further payment to, or for the direct benefit of, such individual under any of the programs specified in subsection (c).

(b) If an institution of higher education determines, after affording notice and opportunity for hearing to an individual attending, or employed by, such institution, that such individual has wilfully refused to obey a lawful regulation or order of such institution after the date of enactment of this Act, and that such refusal was of a serious nature and contributed to a substantial disruption of the administration of such institution, then such institution shall deny, for a period of two years, any further payment to, or for the direct benefit of, such individual under any of the programs specified in subsection (c).

(c) The programs referred to in subsections (a) and (b) are as follows:

(1) The student loan program under title II of the National Defense Education Act of 1958.

(2) The educational opportunity grant program under part A of title IV of the Higher Education Act of 1965.

(3) The student loan insurance program under part B of title IV of the Higher Education Act of 1965.

(4) The college work-study program under part C of title IV of the Higher Education Act of 1965.

(5) Any fellowship program carried out under title II, III, or V of the Higher Education Act of 1965 or title IV or VI of the National Defense Education Act of 1958 . . ."[13]

Such provisions created administrative problems for the agencies administering academic support programs, as well as for the institutions receiving funds under them. For example, the legislative language conflicted with the basic statutory authority of the National Science Foundation and threatened existing NSF policy for supporting controversial individuals which had as its basis the scientific merit of the work of the applicant as judged by his peers. As was the case during the confrontation with Congress in the 1950s, the foundation tried to walk a fine line between conforming with the strict letter of the language and a position that would conciliate between political reality and academic freedom. The foundation's posture was reflected in a statement by Dr. Robert Morison, then a member of the National Science Board:

> The point is that we have moved with great (some would say frightening) rapidity towards the time when virtually all scientific research [is] supported by public funds. . . . These developments mean, among other things, that scientists are in a very real sense wholly dependent on government for their means of livelihood and the pursuit of happiness.
>
> When a young man enters a scientific career these days he makes a substantial investment of time and money on the tacit understanding that he will be provided with a job including a personal salary and facili-

13. See also *National Science Foundation Authorization Act 1970* (P.L. 91-120), 18 November 1969. Section 7 contains a student unrest provision identical with section 504, above, except that the program coverage is limited to "programs authorized by the National Science Foundation Act of 1950; and programs authorized under title IX of the National Defense Education Act of 1958 relating to establishing the Science Information Service."

ties which will vary in amount depending on his demonstrated capacity. By general agreement, factors such as race, religious belief, or political opinion should have nothing to do with his opportunities to support and express himself professionally. Government retains, of course, its usual powers to proceed against a scientist who transgresses the usual laws governing behavior, but the fact that government supports any individual should not give it an additional extra-legal means of denying the inalienable rights enjoyed by all citizens. . . .

Note that the responsibility of government toward the individual scholar is now greater and not less than that of the private university. This is true because of the probability that less damage is done to the individual if a given university discharges him for political reasons than if a government agency denies him a grant. In the former case, he can usually find employment at another, perhaps better institution. The greater responsibility of government stems, in large part from its virtual monopoly position in the support of at least certain areas of science. . . .

To deny access to such support on grounds other than the statutory ones of scientific merit is to act beyond the bounds of due process. Neither the National Science Foundation nor any other granting agency is set up to determine the political guilt or innocence of any individual. This alone should be sufficient reason for leaving such factors aside in assessing proposals. It is reasonably clear that there are many members of the general public, of the press, and even of various parts of the government itself who do not share (this) view. . . . They instinctively turn back to earlier models and think in terms of the pensions, patents, and privileges granted by the sovereign to specially favored individuals, and revocable at will. . . .

In a modern democracy, crucially dependent on a vigorous intellectual life, support of creative activity can no longer be left to such haphazard mechanisms. The establishment of separate agencies such as NSF stemmed from a recognition of the need to support science at the federal level, but in such a way as to separate decisions on scientific merit from the political sensitivities of the sovereign. As trustees of the principle at a time of testing, we must work to define, explain and defend it, even at considerable risk.[14]

The policy of the executive branch regarding the issue eventually was established by President Nixon when he stated his views while approving the 1970 appropriation act for the Departments of State, Justice, and Commerce, the judiciary and related agencies:

> In connection with this provision (Sec. 706) I wish to reaffirm a point I have often made: I do not approve of interference by the federal government in the internal affairs of our colleges and universities.
>
> I am gravely concerned, of course, about the problems of student unrest. At the same time, I have recognized that the enforcement of discipline and maintenance of order in our schools is primarily the responsibility of the schools themselves. The federal government is ill-fitted to play the role of policeman on our college and university campuses.[15]

Notwithstanding President Nixon's disapproval, there was little doubt that Congress intended to interfere in the affairs of the colleges and universities by demanding that they identify persons who had engaged in proscribed conduct and withhold federal funds from them. For example, Congressman R. L. F. Sikes, in explaining the purpose of Section 706 of P.L. 91-153 stated: "it is the intent of the language in Section 706 to tighten

14. "Reflections on Principle" (Unpublished paper prepared in connection with discussions of the support of controversial individuals by the National Science Foundation, 12 August 1967. On file, Office of the Secretary of the Board, National Science Foundation, Washington, D.C.)

15. Statement of President Richard M. Nixon upon signing P.L. 91-153 into law, 29 December 1969.

Section 706 in the Departments of State, Justice, and Commerce, the Judiciary and Related Agencies Appropriation Act of 1970 (P.L. 91-153) contained the language of the Higher Education Amendments of 1968 and additionally required quarterly reporting by recipient institutions that the institution was in compliance with the act.

the law and to make it very clear that there must be compliance by institutions of higher learning."[16]

With the inauguration of President Nixon, federal government initiative affecting higher education policies was no longer dominated by the White House. But because existing amendments to the Higher Education Act of 1965 did not expire until 1971, there was no great pressure on Congress. Parliamentary maneuverings in the Subcommittee on Higher Education, chaired by Congresswoman Edith Green,were aimed at the prevention of further legislation that would deal even more harshly with issues of campus unrest. These were successful and, in the Ninety-second Congress, action on higher education legislation was held over until the second session (1972).

President Nixon indicated his views on higher education policies and programs early in 1970. On 26 January he appeared on nationwide television to veto the HEW appropriation bill, insisting that the increased funds provided by the Congress, for the most part, simply meant more dollars for the same old education programs without making the urgent new reforms that he perceived as being needed. In March, the president forwarded to Congress the first presidential message dealing solely with higher education, calling for a shift in federal spending to emphasize the needs of economicaly poor students and proposing the establishment of a National Foundation for Higher Education, essentially in the image of the National Science Foundation.[17] These proposals, in addition to one recommending the establishment of the National Institute of Education (NIE) to further research and development in education, were to be repeated by President Nixon in a special message in February 1971, in his State of the Union Message in January 1972, and in a January 1974 special message on education.

Although legislation establishing NIE was passed in 1972,[18] other White House recommendations for higher education found

16. *Congressional Record,* 24 July 1969, H6277.

17. Special Message to the Congress on Higher Education, 19 March 1970.

18. The roots of the National Institute of Education go back to the Cooperative Research Program of the Office of Education, established in 1945. For the history of the trials and tribulations of NIE, which continue, see Lee

little support either in Congress or in the higher education community. President Nixon's proposal to establish a National Foundation for Higher Education met with a negative response from college and university administrators.[19] Subsequent action taken by the president in January 1973 which abolished the Office of Science and Technology brought relations between the White House and the academic community to their lowest point in the Nixon period.

In Congress, deliberations on amendments to the Higher Education Act of 1965 snagged over the concept of general aid to colleges and universities, to assist them with operating expenses as an expression of concern for institutional financial health. The breadth of these hearings, and the widespread response from institutions of higher education to them, clearly indicated that the power base for shaping higher education policies had moved from the executive to the legislative branch.[20]

The Quest for Institutional Support

As a part of President Johnson's "better things tò come," a goal pursued assiduously by representatives of higher educa-

Sproull, Stephen Weiner, and David Wolf, *Organizing an Anarchy: Belief, Bureaucracy, and Politics in the National Institute of Education* (Chicago: University of Chicago Press, 1978).

19. For a discussion of the NFHE and the higher education leadership (and a rather harsh indictment of the leadership) see Daniel P. Moynihan, "State vs. Academe," *Harpers* 261 (December 1980): 31–40.

20. A detailed discussion of the sources of policy ideas preceding the 1972 Higher Education Amendments is contained in Wolanin and Gladieux, *Congress and the Colleges,* 43–56. It was a very "yeasty" period in the development of ideas about how the federal government should proceed with the support of higher education. Along with the two basic alternatives of institutional grants and student aid, there were also strong proponents of block grants to the states and for support via tax legislation.

The dominance of the Congress in higher education policy is illustrated by repeated overrides of President Ford's vetoes of appropriation bills for education programs. The only significant initiative by President Ford that affected the higher education community was his recommendation for the reestablishment of a science policy advisory mechanism. The National Science and Technology Policy Organization and Priorities Act of 1976 created the Office of Science and Technology Policy to replace the abolished Office of Science and Technology.

tion in Washington during the mid- and late 1960s was some
form of unrestricted institutional aid for colleges and universities. As we have noted, special forms of institutional support
had been initiated in the early sixties by the National Science
Foundation and the National Institutes of Health. But these
grants were limited to the general support of science functions
and their size was in modest proportion to the amount of research funds awarded to the institutions by the respective agencies. By 1969, NSF institutional grants were broadened to
encompass, on a proportional formula basis, science support
to institutions from all government agencies except the Public
Health Service.[21] At the same time Congressman George Miller,
chairman of the House Committee on Science and Astronautics, had introduced a bill aimed at providing support for science and science education functions in colleges and universities
through a program of institutional grants based on a formula
to be administered by the National Science Foundation.[22] Although neither this nor several subsequent versions of Mr.
Miller's bill were ever enacted, their introduction marked an
important crossing of the pathways of academic science policy
with more general higher education policy, but the pathways
did not merge. Had they done so, it is possible that some of
the confusion and conflict in the policy areas linking government, academic science, and higher education might have been
resolved.[23]

Representatives of the American Council on Education's
Commission on Federal Relations, while stating the council's
support of the Miller Bill, indicated that it was preparing its
own plan for general institutional grants to colleges and universities. The plan corresponded in its essential features to the

21. The program of NSF institutional grants was phased out in December
1974 by executive branch budgetary review in the Office of Mangement and
Budget.

22. Subcommittee on Science, Research, and Development, House Committee on Science and Astronautics, *Hearings on "Institutional Grant Bill,"*
H.R. 35 (subsequently H.R. 11542), 91st Congress, 1st sess., February 1969.

23. For a full discussion of this problem see John T. Wilson, "A Dilemma
of American Science and Higher Education Policy," *Minerva* 9, no. 2 (April
1971): 171–196.

Higher Education General Assistance Bill, which was introduced in the House by Congressman Albert H. Quie in 1970.[24]
The purpose of this bill was to provide institutional grants to
colleges and universities to be determined by formula and administered by the Office of Education.

Mr. Quie's bill fared no better than did those of Mr. Miller.
In the Education Amendments of 1972 and in those that followed in 1976 and 1980, Congress turned its back on institutional aid as a principal means of support for higher education.
Instead, it greatly expanded and elaborated the federal government commitment to student aid. The choice of student aid
may have been academic, inasmuch as the constitutional issue
of direct institutional assistance to church-related schools might
have been an insurmountable difficulty in any test reaching the
courts following the passage of legislation to initiate such support. But it was essentially the inability of those within the
higher education community to come to an agreement on a
basis for distribution of institutional support that influenced the
behavior of congressional authorities, leading them to adopt
the student-aid mode through which the federal government
would provide major support for higher education.[25] Thus by
1978, the end of the second decade following NDEA, the "better things to come" in the federal government's support of
higher education, while growing in total dollar level, were over-
whelmingly (by five-sixths of the increase) in the form of support for students rather than support for categorical programs
or support of institutions.

24. Higher Education General Assistance Act of 1970, H.R. 16622, 24 March
1970. This bill was supplanted by New Comprehensive Education Bill of 1970,
H.R. 18849, 6 August 1970, following hearings on the original bill. H.R. 18849
omits the section of H.R. 16622 covering institutional grants because of the
lack of bipartisan support for the section. See *Congressional Record*, 6 August
1970, E7401, for Mr. Quie's remarks upon introducing H.R. 18849.

25. Congressman John Brademas, former chairman of the Subcommittee on
Post-secondary Education of the House Committee on Education and Labor
is quoted in Moynihan, "State vs. Academe," as saying: "We turned to the
citadel of reason—we said 'tell us what you need' and they answered, 'We
need $150 per student because that is what we've been able to agree upon' "
(38).

Student Aid as the Vehicle of Choice

Although not motivated by concerns for higher education as such, the federal government had earlier established itself as a provider of student aid through the Social Security legislation of New Deal days, through the GI Bill, and through the 1964 Poverty Program. Student aid under these auspices had taken the following forms:

1. Dependents of social security beneficiaries who were unmarried, full-time students were entitled to continue receiving child insurance benefits until the end of the academic year in which they reached the age of twenty-two. Based on the parent's entitlement, the benefits to the student were calculated as one-half the parent's if the latter was retired or disabled, three-quarters if the parent was dead. (Social Security Amendments of 1965.)

2. The GI Bill provided a flat monthly allowance for up to forty-five months of schooling undertaken within ten years of discharge. The program changed for men and women entering the Armed Forces after 1 January 1977. After that date, those who wanted benefits had to contribute to a fund for a minimum of twelve months, which entitled them to matching support from the Veterans' administration at the rate of two to one. (Originally enacted under the Serviceman's Readjustment Act of 1964, the present program was authorized by the Veterans' Readjustment Benefits Act of 1966 and amended by the Veterans' Education and Employment Assistance Act of 1976.)

3. College Work-Study assistance initiated in 1964 by the Economic Opportunity Act gave part-time employment to students enrolled at least half-time, with the government paying up to 80 percent of the student's salary, the employer 20 percent. Eligibility was based on financial need as

assessed by the college or university, and allocations of funds were provided to the institutions
upon application rather than to the student
directly.

As a part of the thrust for direct support of higher education,
the National Defense Education Act of 1958 contained the first
broad-range support for students in the form of educational
loans (for which undergraduates and graduate students were
eligible) and graduate fellowships, in virtually any field, for
students intending to teach at the elementary, secondary, or
higher educational level. The loans themselves—National Defense Student Loans—had cancellation clauses for graduates
going into teaching. The fellowships, as originally authorized,
have since disappeared, and the loans, as a result of various
amendments, have lost their relationsip to teaching and subsequently became "Direct" instead of "Defense" loans.

The Higher Education Act of 1965 moved the federal government further along the road to direct support of higher education. Considered by many as the cornerstone for higher
education policies as they existed up to the time of the Reagan
election, the act provided, along with programs for community
assistance, college library aid, support for "developing" institutions and the National Teachers Corps, two additional forms
of student aid:

1. Supplemental Education Opportunity Grants,
   originally established as Educational Opportunity
   Grants, provided need-based scholarships to undergraduate students.[26] The maximum grant has
   increased through the years, but as with the College Work-Study program, SEOGs are awarded
   to the Student by the institution which must in
   turn apply each year to the federal government
   for an allocation of funds.

2. Guaranteed Student Loans for which the principal was to come from the private sector—banks,

26. Amounts of awards and conditions of awards are subject to change with
new amendments and regulations.

savings and loan institutions, and occasionally
universities themselves. The principal was "guaranteed" against default by the federal government, and the interest was subsidized by the
government while the borrower was enrolled in
school if he came from a family with an income
below $18,000. Interest was originally set at 7
percent, but to encourage private lenders the
government paid them a special fee beyond the
interest rate. The Middle Income Student Assistance Act of 1978 removed any income ceiling
for loan eligibility and for interest subsidy, with
predictable expansionary results.

In choosing student aid as its primary vehicle, the 1972 Higher
Education Amendments clarified, to some extent, existing federal policy for support of higher education. But at the same
time, the amendments confused even further the student aid
effort, as they authorized three new programs, not as replace-
ments to older ones, but as additions.

1. Basic Educational Opportunity Grants: This program was especially significant for two reasons—
it was an entitlement program (guaranteeing "access" to college in the words of its sponsors) and
the student applied directly for aid under the program rather than through his college. Limited to
undergraduates, the BEOGs were need-based
and were intended to provide up to 50 percent of
a student's college costs or a set dollar maximum, whichever was less. The largest scholarship program by far, the BEOGs[27] were explicitly
intended to be the foundation upon which all
other federal student assistance to undergraduates was based. Congress insisted, however, on a
"trigger" mechanism by which the BEOG program could not be funded unless the earlier

27. Renamed Pell Grants in 1980 after Senator Claiborne Pell of Rhode
Island, chairman of the Subcommittee on Education of the Senate Committee
on Labor and Public Welfare and a leading sponsor of higher education legislation.

SEOG and CWS programs were funded to a certain level.

2. State Student Incentive Grants: Important as a first, modest, and lonely effort to relate federal student assistance to the relatively new state scholarship programs. To encourage the states to establish their own student aid programs, the SSIGs matched state allocations up to a predetermined level.

3. Formula Institutional Aid: A program aimed at satisfying those constituencies pressing for institutional assistance that was never funded.

All of the existing student aid programs were reauthorized by the Education Amendments of 1976 without change in principle. Pressure was growing, however, for help within the middle-income parents group, who maintained that they were the forgotten people between the poor, who were being assisted, and the rich, who could afford higher education no matter what it would cost. Responsive to such pressure, Congress enacted and President Carter signed the Middle-Income Student Assistance Act of 1978.

The Middle-Income Student Assistance Act and the Higher Education Amendments of 1980 significantly broadened the scope of federal student assistance. MISA extended eligibility for the interest deferred benefits of Guaranteed Student Loans to all students enrolled at least half-time, expanded eligibility for Basic Educational Opportunity Grants (Pell Grants), and increased funding authorizations for most existing student aid programs. The 1980 amendments raised all grant programs' maximum benefit amount, eliminated equity in the family home as a partial determinant of need, and created a new loan program for parents.

The amendments of 1976 and 1980 and the Middle-Income Student Assistance Act added essentially nothing of substance to existing higher educational legislation. With the passage of the 1972 amendments, despite appearances to the contrary, higher education was approaching a sharp decline on the political agenda of the nation. There was growing competition from urban welfare problems, from the civil rights movement, and from other levels of the education system. And to the disillusionments with academic science that were beginning to show was added congressional disenchantment with the parochial interests exhibited by the various components of American higher education. After a decade and a half on center stage, and after enjoying the legislative cornucopia of the Johnson years, higher education and academic science were heading in directions that would render them simply added functions, among many, of the federal government.

Mr. Carter: The Department of Education

Between the years that NDEA was passed and higher education legislation reached its peak, there were not infrequent murmurs regarding the ineffectiveness of the higher education community's representation within the executive branch of government. The American Council on Education, from time to time, had expressed dissatisfaction with the status of the Office of Education within the Department of Health, Education, and Welfare. Within the academic scientific community there was widespread lack of confidence in the competence of the Office of Education to administer effectively programs of any sort, and there was no enthusiasm whatsoever for having science education programs moved under its administrative aegis.

Various suggestions were made to remedy the situation, including elevating the Office of Education to cabinet rank, making the commissioner an under- or assistant secretary, creating a National Board of Education, and, as proposed by President Nixon, creating a national foundation along lines parallel to the National Science Foundation. A strong political thrust for a Department of Education was mounted through efforts of the National Education Association in the early 1970s, and a number of bills were introduced in the Congress, without success of enactment. The idea subsided and languished until the presidential campaign of 1976, when candidate Jimmy Carter indicated his support for a Department of Education.

The creation of a Department of Education was one of the highest legislative priorities during President Carter's first two years in office and, in a special message on education in February 1978, he informed the Congress:

> I have instructed the Office of Management and Budget and the Department of Health, Education and Welfare to work with Congress on legislation needed to establish a Department of Education which will:
>
> let us focus on Federal educational policy at the highest levels of our government;
>
> permit closer coordination of Federal education programs and other related activities;
>
> reduce Federal regulations and reporting requirements and cut duplication;
>
> assist school districts, teachers, and parents to make better use of local resources and ingenuity.
>
> A separate Cabinet-level department will enable the Federal government to be a true partner with State, local and private education institutions in sustaining and improving the quality of our education system.[28]

On 17 October 1979 President Carter signed into law legislation creating a Department of Education.[29] The creation of the new department, in his words, signaled "a significant milestone in my effort to make the federal government more effective. We will now have a single cabinet department which can provide the coherence and sense of direction needed to manage billions of dollars in U.S. education funds."[30]

28. Message to the Congress, *Congressional Record*, 28 February 1978, S2512.

29. Department of Education Organization Act (P.L. 96-88), 17 October 1979. For a brief summary of events leading to the creation of the Department of Education, see Finn, *Scholars, Dollars, and Bureaucrats*, 193ff.

30. *Washington Post*, 28 September 1979, 1.

Viewed within the context of federal education policy, the creation of the department was largely a response by both the president and the Congress to the National Education Association.[31] Certainly there was nothing in the legislative action which could be interpreted as congressional authorization for significant new initiatives for education on the part of the federal government. The department amalgamated a part, but only a part, of existing education programs and functions.[32] It is indeed difficult to see how it ever could have realized President Carter's hope for "coherence and sense of direction" within the various programs that support higher education.

The 1980 election, of course, shattered any expectation that the new department would achieve the goals of its chief architect. It had barely gotten organized before it became responsible to a new president. And in his campaign rhetoric, President Reagan had promised, along with other actions aimed at getting the affairs of the nation back in order, the Department of Education's early demise.

November 1980: Cracks in the "Consensus"

During the two decades prior to the presidential election of 1980, higher education policies that had led to NDEA and subsequent education legislation, had been shaped by a national political consensus—frequently referred to as "education's liberal consensus"—that had roots going back to Franklin Roosevelt's New Deal. As characterized by Chester Finn, the

31. See Rufus E. Miles, Jr., "A Cabinet Department of Education: An Unwise Campaign Promise or a Sound Idea?" *Public Administration Review* 39, no. 2 (March/April 1979): 103–10.

32. Programs moved to the new department, as provided in the act, included the Education Division of HEW, encompassing elementary, secondary and postsecondary education programs and research activities; the education-related activities of the Office of Civil Rights; the Overseas Dependents' Schools of the Department of Defense; the law enforcement student loan programs of the Department of Justice; the College Housing Loan Program of the Department of Housing and Urban Development; the Migrant Education program of Labor; the Special institutions for which HEW exercised budgetary oversight, including Howard University, Gallaudet College, the American Printing House for the Blind, and the National Technical Institute for the Deaf; The Telecommunications Non-Broadcast Demonstration Program, HEW; and that portion

liberal consensus included representatives from a broad band
of political and social institutions: the major private foundations, such as Ford and Carnegie; the elite universities; the
major national organizations of teachers and educational institutions (the National Education Association and the American Council on Education, for example); various civil rights
groups; most of the industrial labor unions; the intellectual
think-tanks, such as Brookings and the Aspen Institute; and
various individuals from the executive branch, the Congress,
and the more-influential newspapers, including the *New York
Times* and the *Washington Post*.[33] Names associated with the
liberal consensus which by 1980 had become educational
household words included Clark Kerr, Ernest Boyer, Stephen
Bailey, Harold ("Doc") Howe, and Samuel Halperin.

Although not reflecting unanimity at all times (the issue of
a Department of Education caused severe strains within the
consensus), the major goals and principles shaping policies in
support of higher education by the federal government emphasized growth of those items in the federal budget that would
enhance institutional and individual support to ensure availability to all who might benefit from higher education; legislation to guarantee equal access to educational opportunities;
desegregation of the higher education enterprise in all respects,
including race, sex, and age; support for scholarly functions
in areas ranging from the sciences to the humanities and arts;
and, perhaps most important, a vigorous activist posture on
the part of the federal government, utilizing regulatory and legal
procedures to attain all of the programmatic ends that flowed
from such policies. Within these major themes, minor and

---

of the precollegiate science education programs of the National Science Foundation having to do with science-teacher development and minority institutions
science improvement.

A number of programs were omitted from the legislation because of opposition within the constituencies having strong ties with various departments
and agencies which control the programs. The most significant of these were
the veterans' education programs, job training, Head Start, and the major
portion of the science education effort of the National Science Foundation.

33. Chester E. Finn, Jr., "The Future of Education's Liberal Consensus,"
Change 12, no. 16 (September 1980): 25–30.

sometimes parochial variations emphasized "innovation and reform," life-long learning, and aspirations for a better relationship between federally sponsored and state-based higher education programs. Finn has aptly summarized the essence of the liberal consensus as reflecting:

> a near boundless confidence in the ability of the national
> government to deploy its resources in ways that reduce
> the educational consequences of individual differences.
> It (the consensus) sought to weaken the correlation be-
> tween income and educational opportunity, and to give
> more people a chance at more education than would
> have been the case if the federal government had kept
> out of the field.[34]

On the whole, and over a significant period of time, the objectives and policies espoused by the liberal consensus were acceptable to a broad spectrum of individuals within the colleges and universities. The efforts that created and sustained a wide variety of programs so increased the flow of funds to essentially all institutions that traditionally conflicting issues, purposes, and goals were kept in check. But, as with all loosely structured political and social alliances as they grow older and more demanding with success, by the time the presidential election of 1980 rolled around, significant cracks were beginning to show in the interfaces between the membership of the consensus. It had, in Finn's words, "begun to grow greedy, smug, extreme and, at the same time, defensive."[35]

The issue which caused the most severe strain was one that had surfaced from time to time, but which had always been rationalized in the interests of harmony. Throughout its history, the consensus had consistently stressed "quantity"—in budgetary growth, in increased numbers of students having access to higher education, in types of support programs available, in minority hirings, and in bureaucratic growth. Over time, and especially in the face of budgets that had reached plateaus and were being diminished by inflation, the qualitative aspects of

34. Ibid., p. 26.
35. Ibid.

higher education were being more closely examined by politicians, by the citizenry, and by educators themselves. Among the elements that increasingly differentiated the quantitative and the qualitative viewpoints were the question of educational equity and equality in contrast to an emphasis on quality; the role and use of objective measures of program and student achievement; differing attitudes toward the concept of "accountability" with respect to the use of resources; the trend toward homogenization of institutions as opposed to the maintenance of pluralism and diversity, especially the attitude toward programs and institutions that might reflect "elitism"; the proper role of government in solving education problems and in the administration of regulatory mechanisms; the ever-present problem of "quotas" and the related problem of "reverse discrimination"; and, finally, the role of educators themselves in the complex relationships between the federal government and higher education.

Regardless of the outcome of the presidential election—indeed had there been no election in 1980—the agenda facing the higher education community at that time reflected serious stresses and strains which were not only political, but reflected issues that were cultural and social in nature. Politically, it was not obvious from the platform or rhetoric of either of the major candidates that education in general or higher education in particular would enjoy a high priority among the problems facing the country in the four years of his prospective incumbency. Furthermore, the legislative amendments of 1972 through 1980 were convincing evidence that the center of political power in matters of education policy lay in the Congress, so that prior to the election, it was conceivable that it mattered very little as to who was to be in the White House in 1981.

In the aftermath of President Reagan's dramatic defeat of the incumbent president, those responsible for the future of higher education faced a confused situation. The most obvious question was what kind of policies toward higher education would characterize the new administration. The defeat and retirement of members of Congress who had been strong supporters of higher education programs throughout their terms in office, and the effect of those defeats and retirements on education's congressional power base, complicated the political question. There was also the question of the direction in which higher education should turn. Of very great importance to the prospective posture of higher education was the fact that among those identified with the new conservative political trend were many who prominently identified with higher education: Nathan Glazer, Daniel Bell, Irving Kristol, Sidney Hook, and Peter Drucker, to name but a few. It was largely from these individuals and from others reflecting similar values that the "neoconservative" challenge to the liberal education consensus had grown.

Thus, as the Reagan administration prepared for the transition into office, the situation, both politically and educationally, presaged a contest of values between the quantitative characteristics of existing federal support programs and a firmly expressed concern for the reestablishment of traditional qualitative standards within the education enterprise and a reestablishment of conservative social and economic values in the society.

3

Higher Education

The Reagan Administration

The New Agenda: Economics and the Budget

When President Reagan assumed office on 20 January 1981, federal programs, including those supporting higher education and academic science, were operating on the basis of appropriations made by the Ninety-sixth Congress, recommended by President Carter's budget for fiscal year 1981. The new administration faced the immediate task of submitting to the Ninety-seventh congress, which had just convened, budgetary and legislative agenda based upon its own policies and priorities for coping with the nation's problems. Of first priority were the program and budget recommendations which would (1) modify Carter programs and budgets for fiscal year 1981, and (2) establish President Reagan's program and budgetary goals for fiscal year 1982. The time base was thus the remainder of fiscal year 1981 (20 January 1981–30 September 1981) and the whole of fiscal year 1982 (1 October 1981–30 September 1982).[1]

The outline of the new administration's economic program was presented by President Reagan in an address to a joint session of the Congress on 18 February 1981.[2] The major elements were those he had stressed during the campaign: control of inflation; promotion of economic growth through lightened

1. For a description of congressional procedures for budget review and appropriation action see Alice M. Rivlin, "Congress and the Economy," *Bulletin of the American Academy of Arts and Sciences* 34 (February 1981): 22–36.
2. "A Program for Economic Recovery," 18 February 1981.

tax burdens; reduced government regulation; reduced budget deficits; expanded employment opportunities; and strengthened national defense. The plan reflected a strong faith in the private sector rather than in the federal government as the fundamental source of economic motivation and growth. The plan also proposed to restore state and local government responsibility in areas which the president believed had been usurped in recent years by the federal government. The essence of the message, in the president's words, was "as humanely as possible . . . to move America back toward economic sanity."[3]

All of the major elements of the president's general economic program related in some fashion, directly or indirectly, to the nation's universities and colleges. They were intimately connected with the education and training of individuals whose efforts would affect the economy in diverse ways; they were involved in the advancement of the frontiers of scientific knowledge and its application to the practical problems of an industrial society; they influenced the broad social and cultural goals of the society. The important question was how the new administration would adapt the general policies that made up its economic program to the higher education enterprise (as one of the many segments of the society) through new or modified programs in support of higher education and academic scholarship.

The Reagan Inheritance

The Reagan administration, of course, inherited literally hundreds of programs, large and small, from which federal funds were flowing into the colleges and universities. The principal agencies which had developed over the years to coordinate and control federal support for higher education included (1) the Department of Education, which administers programs for the support of students and for the support of institutions (developing institutions, the land-grant colleges, and special

3. Message to the Congress, *Fiscal Year 1982 Budget Revisions,* 10 March 1981, 1.

institutions for the deaf and blind); (2) the Veterans' Administration and the Social Security Administration, which administer the veterans' readjustment benefit program and social security educational benefits; (3) the agencies supporting major substantive programs, for example, the National Science Foundation, the National Endowments for the Humanities and for the Arts, and the National Institutes of Health. Forms of support from these sources encompass traditional faculty research activities and education programs across all educational levels. Also included within this source are the "mission" agencies (Agriculture, Defense, Energy, for example), whose "categorical" programs usually take the form of research support but not infrequently include programs to support advanced training in "categorical" areas. Finally, there are (4) the Internal Revenue Service, which largely controls support in the form of reduced tax liabilities for students and parents (tax policies that allow deductions for contributions to educational institutions also provide federal assistance in an indirect way to higher education), and (5) the Equal Employment Opportunity Commission and other agencies responsible for enforcement of antidiscrimination legislation and regulations.

Within this complex, the Reagan administration would discover no sense of overall "theory" in higher education policies as developed under prior administrations, although the policies generally reflected three purposes: first, assuring equal educational opportunities for potential students; second, easing the financial burden for families supporting students in colleges and universities; and, third, assisting institutions, in a variety of ways, to sustain fiscal viability and intellectual productivity.[4]

As for the dollar value, because of the organizational scattering of the programs and the diversity of expressed purposes, there was considerable opportunity for error in combining the numerous pieces of the funding jigsaw puzzle. But within an acceptable degree of error, an estimate of the magnitude of the enterprise inherited by the Reagan administration, in annual

4. For details, see the analysis contained in *Postsecondary Education: the Current Federal Role and Alternative Approaches* (Washington, D.C.: Congressional Budget Office, 1977).

budgetary terms, was about $17 billion in support for higher education. Of this, some $10 billion was in the form of student assistance of various kinds, about $4 billion was in payments to institutions (not including funds for federal laboratories managed by educational institutions), and approximately $3 billion was in the form of reduced tax liabilities.[5]

The Reagan Approach to Student Aid

In her testimony before Congress as it was reviewing the funding requirements for higher education programs in fiscal year 1981 and fiscal year 1982, Dr. Alice Rivlin, director of the Congressional Budget Office, pointed out that prior enacted expansions in student eligibility, without increased funding, had reduced the federal commitment to assist the most needy students, while increasing assistance to less needy students. In fiscal year 1980, funds had been withdrawn from the needs-based Pell program to satisfy the demands of the Guaranteed Student Loan program (an entitlement program), because both the demands for loans and interest rates were higher than expected. In addition, the needs-based National Direct Student Loan program had been reduced. Dr. Rivlin patiently explained that before policy could be set for 1981 and beyond, the Congress must resolve these funding issues because "without some change in the current programs, federal student assistance will almost certainly continue to shift away from helping the most needy students."[6]

The American Council on Education, speaking through its Commission on Governmental Relations, had made the same point in presenting its agenda to the Ninety-seventh Congress.

5. This and subsequent references to budget data are taken from *The United States Budget in Brief, Fiscal Year 1981; Fiscal Year 1982 Budget Revisions, March 1981; The United States Budget in Brief, Fiscal Years 1983 and 1984*— all issued by the Executive Office of the President, Office of Management and Budget, Washington—and from unpublished data from the Congressional Budget Office, June 1981.

6. Testimony of Alice M. Rivlin, 11 May 1981 before the Subcommittee on Education, Arts, and Humanities, Committee on Labor and Human Resources, United States Senate.

Reaching the goal of full funding of the authorization for student aid programs contained in the Higher Education Amendments of 1980, it said, "is the highest priority of the higher education community."[7]

The Heritage Foundation Report, which was generally considered the most likely source for clues about the direction of the new administration's policies, recommended that the administration aim at a new system of financing that would relieve the higher education enterprise of its dependence upon direct governmental financing—thus reducing the continuing threat of government control.[8] As specifically applied to student aid programs, the policy would translate into budget and administrative actions that would emphasize direct payments to the neediest students or their families, minimize payments to institutions, and place expanded responsibilities on the private sector of the economy (the individual and his family) for funding higher education.

In March 1981, the Reagan administration transmitted to the Congress a proposal for "Certain Amendments to the Higher Education Act of 1965." The draft bill included several items relating to the administrative authority of the secretary of education and items that would affect the new program for parental loans (initiated in only the state of Massachusetts at that time). The core of the proposed legislation was aimed at modifying the Pell Grant program, the Supplemental Education Opportunity grants and Guaranteed Student Loans.

If enacted, the Reagan amendments of 1981 would have provided that a student's Pell Grant could not exceed the difference between the student's cost of attendance and the sum of the student's expected family contribution and the amount of expected self-help, as determined by the secretary. The self-help requirement could be waived if the aid administrator determined that the limitation would cause severe financial hardship. The self-help requirement would have been applied to Supple-

7. "A Higher Education Agenda for the 97th Congress." *Educational Record* 62 (Spring 1981): 9–17.
8. *Mandate for Leadership*. (Washington, D.C.: 1980). The Heritage Foundation.

mental Educational Opportunity Grants as well as to the traditional family contribution assessed on the basis of its
resources, although, again, this requirement could be waived
if the aid administrator determined that it would cause severe
financial hardship. The proposed amendments limited the
amount of any Guaranteed Student Loans made after 30 June
1981 to a student's remaining need—educational costs minus
all other aid, the expected family contributions, and self-help.
Moreover, they eliminated the provision in legislation which
allowed the GSL to replace expected family contributions and
required need determination for GSL to be calculated under
the Federal Need Analysis System. Under the Parent Loan
program, the Reagan bill allowed a GSL to be counted as part
of the student's expected family contribution in the determination of need, but no loans could be made to any parent or
student which would cause their combined loans for any academic year to exceed the student's estimated cost of attendance minus the student's estimated financial assistance. The
in-school interest subsidy and postschool repayment grace period for GSLs borrowed after 1 July 1981 were to be eliminated,
as were administrative cost allowances allowed institutions under existing programs.

The fiscal 1982 budget revisions to Congress supported the
proposed legislation. The rhetoric accompanying both the draft
bill and the budget revisions carried assurances that the "truly
needy" student would not be negatively affected. It pointed
out that although the original purpose of the Pell Grant program
had been to assist low-income students, later amendments to
higher education legislation had allowed for grants to students
from families with income in excess of $30,000 per year (there
was no income limitation, in fact, although awards were need
based). The recommendations also proposed to target Pell
Grants more specifically to the "truly needy" (presumably to
families with income below $30,000), by increasing the amount
of discretionary income that families must contribute to the
support of a student, and by requiring $750 self-help contri-
bution from students, except where extreme financial need is

demonstrated.[9] The changes in Pell Grants and others in the GSL program were aimed at students and families that had taken advantage of the very liberal eligibility rules in existing student aid programs to obtain grants and loans, thereby allowing them to invest their own funds at high rates of return while paying for their higher education with government funds borrowed at a lower rate.[10]

Another budget recommendation proposed that, starting in fiscal 1982, benefits to students whose parents were Social Security beneficiaries would no longer be available to newly eligible recipients. Payments would be phased out by reductions of 25 percent annually for students still receiving such benefits. The principal rationale underlying this proposal was that such payments duplicated benefits available under other federal student assistance programs.[11]

As the House Education and Labor Committee took action on the student loan portion of the fiscal 1982 education authorization bill, Congressman Peter A. Peyser announced dramatically: "Today may be remembered by hundreds of thousands of students around the country as the Pearl Harbor day of education in the United States."[12] In attempting to meet

9. *FY 1982 Budget Revisions,* 65.

10. In 1981 roughly 20 percent of all aid went to students from families with incomes over $30,000 (Rivlin Testimony, 10 March 1982, Subcommittee on Postsecondary Education, Committee on Education and Labor, U.S. House of Representatives).

11. *FY 1982 Budget Revisions,* 75. Two other administration actions relating to student assistance are of interest and reflect the strength of its commitment to the president's economic recovery program. First, as a part of the effort to gain control of the "credit budget" the Department of Education's guarantees of obligations of the Student Loan Marketing Association were decreased in fiscal 1982 and terminated thereafter "to curtail further use of off-budget financing through the Federal Financing Bank." The Student Loan Marketing Association's financial condition was sufficiently strong, in the president's view, to "go wholly private thereafter."

Second, although the concept of "tuition-tax credit" was highlighted in both platform and campaign rhetoric, the administration has not pushed for such legislation. Testimony in support of the Packwood-Moynihan bill was only modestly supportive. Economic problems have first priority. Consistently following elections, presidential candidates have shied away from tuition credit programs because of their diminution of tax revenue.

12. *New York Times,* 11 June 1981, 1.

the budget constraints recommended to the Congress by the president's 1982 budget revisions and established by the first concurrent budget resolutions for that fiscal year, both House and Senate education committees were forced to adopt authorizing legislation which would, among other things, result in reduced authorization for Pell Grants, reduced volume for student loan programs, reduced subsidies for interest during the period of loans, increased rates on parental and student loans, increased levels for family contributions to student expenses, and the elimination of administrative allowances to institutions for administering loan programs.

Appropriation actions in Congress on the various bills authorized by the Omnibus Budget Reconciliation Act for 1982 were delayed until after the August recess. During this period, various economic signs continued to be unfavorable and, as Congress returned to work in September, it faced a declining stock market, continued high interest rates, and a revised federal budget projection which estimated an increased deficit. The president faced the alternatives of either failing to meet his budgetary goals, including a balanced federal budget by 1984, or making further cuts in an already sharply reduced budget for fiscal 1982.

Since the latter was chosen, the question then became one of where the cuts should be made. White House sentiment favored additional cuts in social programs, with token cuts in the defense budget. But congressional leaders indicated strong reluctance to accept the proposed White House course of action. On 24 September, the president made a nationally televised talk, presenting his plans for further budget reductions in the interest of meeting his economic and budget goals. These included, among other things, a further reduction of some 12 percent in appropriations for most government agencies (except defense) and a sharp reduction in government employment. The president also reiterated his plan to abolish the Department of Education.

Congress responded with a 4 percent across-the-board reduction in most domestic programs, while slightly increasing appropriations for agriculture and defense. Appropriation bills for the majority of agencies and departments were signed by the president during the 1981 Christmas holiday period, but because the bill for the Department of Education was delayed, a "continuing resolution" was passed as authority for maintaining education programs through 31 March 1982, which was subsequently renewed to keep programs running through the remainder of the fiscal year.

In the meantime, the president's fiscal 1983 budget proposed further significant reductions in the Pell Grants program, including increasing stringencies for grant eligibility; elimination of funds for Supplemental Educational Opportunity Grants, National Direct Student Loans, and State Student Incentive Grants; denial of access by graduate students to Guaranteed Student Loans, and curtailment of interest subsidies to other recipients of guaranteed loans; and elimination of the graduate fellowship programs of the Department of Education that primarily aided women and minority groups.[13] The total request for the student aid programs of the Department of Education for fiscal 1983 was approximately $1.8 billon, compared to $3.57 billon for fiscal 1982. Guaranteed Student Loans were budgeted at $2.48 billion for 1983, compared to $3.07 the year before, but the restricted access to the program was eliminated.

In a continuing resolution, the Congress in December 1982 approved a $15 billion appropriation for the Department of Education for fiscal year 1983. This was a slight increase from the $14.6 billion level of 1982. The total included some $6.6 billion for student aid programs for academic year 1983–84, with the College Work-Study program showing a slight increase and the State Student Incentive effort a slight decrease. In February 1983, the Office of Management and Budget countered with a proposal to rescind about $1.5 billion in higher education funds for fiscal 1983 because of the need for fiscal stringency.

13. See *Chronicle of Higher Education,* 8 December 1982, 12 for a detailed comparison by program in: 1982, president's budget for 1982, and Congressional action for 1983. In the budget as submitted, graduate and professional students could borrow only under the much less subsidized "auxiliary" loan program administered through the states.

In his 1984 budget, President Reagan proposed keeping student assistance programs at their current levels, with the introduction of a new self-help program being created from the Pell, the Supplemental Educational Opportunity, and the State Student Incentive Grants programs.[14] Under the self-help concept, the student was expected to pay 40 percent or $800 of his or her school costs, whichever was greater. The education budget also contained a savings plan to encourage parents to save money for their children's college education based upon avoidance of taxes on interest and dividends. The total request of $13.2 billion for the Department of Education reflected a modified administration attitude toward student assistance as a necessary and perhaps a good thing, and a concession to congressional action which had consistently rejected severe reductions in these programs. In the absence of administration proposals for cuts in student aid budgets in the president's 1984 budget, the probability that Congress will take action to alter the programs substantively is not high. The most likely time to look for substantive change in the higher education programs is when Congress begins work on the reauthorization of the Higher Education Act in 1985.[15]

Higher Education: Midterm Trial Balance

Beyond what may be gained from analyses of the annual jousting on the president's budgets, we see the Reagan administration's view of the relationship between the federal government and higher education most clearly reflected in statements made by the secretary of education, Terrel H. Bell.

14. Details are included in the Presidential Message on Education dated 7 March 1983.

15. We have limited our discussion of the support of higher education essentially to the major program areas, i.e., student aid, the sciences, and the arts and humanities. The reader should be aware that there are additional programs, albeit relatively minor in dollar levels of support: for example, college library grants, international education, the National Institute of Education, and grants to states for higher education planning and for continuing education. Total continuing spending authority for the Department of Education's programs in higher education was approximately $7 billion for 1982–83.

In an interview during the summer of 1981, Secretary Bell indicated that he hoped to reverse the trend toward federal control of education while at the same time making federal dollars responsive to state and local needs. Responding to a question about the government's "appropriate role," it was the secretary's view that

> the federal government's most important role is ensuring access of students to higher education. Most of the federal money goes to providing opportunities for students who could not otherwise afford to attend college. Federal aid also gives them access to institutions of their choice. Student aid continues to be the Department of Education's first priority—it has been a priority of previous administrations, and certainly will continue to be emphasized by this administration. We should also try to help redress nationwide weaknesses in higher education; programs such as Title III of the Higher Education Act help to strengthen developing colleges and universities—another role of the federal government.
>
> An additional role is to sponsor research essential to the nation's security and to the productivity and economic competitiveness of our country. Research is essential to the welfare, well-being, and prosperity of the American people. Much of this research is not sponsored by the Department of Education, yet is still part of the federal government's role in higher education. Surely that activity ought to be continued. The government ought to refrain from doing anything that will encroach on the autonomy of institutions and their governing boards. I fear the government has been indulging in the opposite of that behavior lately. The Reagan administration is committed to state and local control of education and to institutional independence and autonomy in both public and private institutions. I hope we can do more in that regard, and maybe with more thought and deliberation, refrain from encroaching upon the rights and prerogatives and the traditions of autonomy that our institutions enjoy.[16]

16. *Educational Record* 62 (Summer 1981): 5.

In August 1981, with the 1982 budget actions out of the way, Secretary Bell submitted to the president an "option paper" recommending that the Department of Education be abolished in favor of a new organizational form. The paper contained four options: (1) merging the department into another, existing department; (2) dispersing the department's functions among several departments and placing an education advisor on the White House staff; (3) creating an "independent agency" at subcabinet level; and (4) converting the existing department into a "national Education Foundation," in the image of the National Science Foundation. The last of the four was the one recommended by the secretary.

Subsequently, President Reagan's budget for fiscal 1983 incorporated a plan for transforming the department into a subcabinet level education foundation. The plan suggested transfer of some education programs to other agencies and departments but retention of the department's student aid programs within the foundation. As conceived, the foundation would be a new federal education agency devoted largely to student aid, research, and to gathering educational statistics. However, there was less than overwhelming enthusiasm in Congress as it pursued budget action to abolish the department, and there has been no evidence to date to suggest that the administration can mount sufficient voting strength to do so.

Although the Reagan administration has failed to realize its goal of reducing the higher education budget significantly, program dollar levels are of less importance than are the facts of the attempted reductions, along with other actions to tighten eligibility standards for participation in student aid programs and to increase requirements for family contribution to college costs. Clearly, through its budget recommendations and related actions, the Reagan administration has set a course to re-establish the traditional view that the primary responsibility for the costs of higher education should rest with the student and his family. When family support is not available under strict limiting conditions, presumably the government will help the needy segment of the student population. For the rest of the student population, the administration rejects the two-decade liberal consensus that called for a partnership of family-school-government in financing a student's education but that had, in President Reagan's view, too generously shared government funds in the cost of financing higher education.

To meet proposed federal government reductions in student assistance, several states have developed programs to pick up at least some of the slack. However, most states are caught in their own budgetary squeeze and, like the federal government, are tightening the qualification requirements for state scholarships. Thus as the colleges and universities shape their own student aid programs, they are dealing with student and family constituencies that are newly ineligible for federal and state grants or that will receive smaller amounts of assistance because of increased standards for parental conributions or student self-help.[17]

It is not surprising that directors of admission and deans of students generally agree with Congressman Peyser's Pearl Harbor metaphor. At the same time, the results of the various cuts will not become clear for at least another school year or two. There is little doubt that the increased financial difficulties of school attendance, both at the undergraduate and graduate levels, will serve to enhance the role of motivational factors, resulting in the survival of students who are determined to obtain higher education despite the absence of easily obtainable government support. One is reminded that prior to the expansion of assistance programs in the 1960s, students did obtain undergraduate and advanced degrees because they were determined to be college graduates, or humanists or scientists, regardless of financial conditions. And it is also true that even under recent conditions of very generous support programs, the difference between the amount of assistance available to graduate students in the humanities and those in the sciences was significant. It may well be that, in the absence of agreement on any other basis among those responsible for higher education, the "budget" will be the instrument through which

17. For an excellent review of the situation as of autumn 1982, see "Financial Aid Offices Float New Strategies." *New York Times Education Supplement,* 12 November 1982.

standards of quality will be restored. But it also is possible that the administration's actions will lead to a set of conditions wherein children of the wealthy will have their choice of schools, the children of the poor will have access only to less expensive schools, and the children of middle-income families will be left to scramble for either choice or access as best they can.

4

The Reagan Administration
and the
Substantive Programs

The Humanities and the Arts

Early in February 1981, a story in the Washington Post, presumably reflecting the views of President Reagan's director of the Office of Management and Budget, indicated that both the National Endowment for the Arts and the National Endowment for the Humanities were candidates for extinction.[1] Neither, in his reported judgment, had claims for funding from the federal government. However, in contrast to this view, the Heritage Foundation transition report took a positive stand with reference to the missions of both endowments, stating that any administration, whether it be Democratic, Republican or Independent, ought to have no difficulty in accepting the proposition that the encouragement and support of national progress in the humanities and arts are appropriate matters of concern to the federal government. The report went on to assert that federal government support for the arts and humanities is crucial if the country is to maintain any degree of leadership, not only in science and technology, but, as it put it, in the realm of ideas and the spirit.

From the point of view of colleges and universities, the Heritage Report made the important recommendation that NEH should put greater emphasis on support of research, presumably at the expense of programs aimed at public education,

1. *Washington Post,* 5 February 1981, 1.

especially at secondary school curricula and teacher education. In a similar vein, in discussing the budget of the Arts Endowment, it was critical of education programs. However, in both cases, changes were to be obtained by restructuring programs, and it was recommended that fiscal 1982 budgets remain at fiscal 1981 levels.

But the new administration's budget actions, in both the fiscal 1981 and the fiscal 1982 revisions, did not support this recommendation. After early reports of rather drastic recisions in fiscal programs, President Reagan requested and received reductions of $7.4 million from the $151 million appropriated funds for the Humanities Endowment and $6.65 million from the $159 million of the Arts Endowment. However, in the 1982 budget revisions, substantial cuts were recommended by the President, to a level of $85 million for the Humanities Endowment and $88 million for the Arts Endowment. In explaining the proposed reductions, the administration pointed out that historically these kinds of activities have been maintained by state and local support, including the philanthropy of individuals and corporations. In the actions proposed, the administration was aiming at restoring the historic reliance on nonfederal sources.[2]

But both the House and the Senate committees were of a different mind from the president, presenting bills to their respective colleagues which recommended for both endowments appropriations beyond the $100 million level. Following the September request by the president for additional budget reductions, Congress approved budget cuts for the two endowments by trimming 4 percent from the appropriations bill drafted earlier by a House-Senate conference committee. The amended bill provided $130.6 million in fiscal 1982 for the Humanities Endowment, compared with the $151.3 million provided in fiscal 1981. The Arts Endowment received $143 million in 1982, as compared to the $158.8 million level of 1981.

Subsequent to his recommendations on the 1982 budget, President Reagan appointed two task forces charged with

2. *FY 1982 Budget Revisions,* 65.

studying and making recommendations regarding both appropriate form and substance in the relationships between the federal government and the arts and humanities. The administration requested that responses be available by early autumn 1981. The reports, submitted in late September, reaffirmed the two endowments as appropriate structures through which public support should be conveyed to the arts and humanities. The task forces found the endowments to be "basically sound" and recommended that they remain as conceived in their enabling legislation. Among the various other recommendations having to do with the structure of the advisory council and with program activities, perhaps the most important, in the light of the Reagan administration's economic and tax policies, stressed the need for improved leadership in both the public and the private sectors if potential supporters were to be encouraged to give to the arts and humanities.[3]

Regardless of the favorable reports, in the president's budget for fiscal 1983, both the Humanities and the Arts Endowments were faced with reductions. But as was the case in the year before, Congress disagreed with the president and appropriated funds for each agency at the same level as for fiscal 1982. In something of an instant replay, the 1984 budget again recommended reductions in both endowments: $112.2 million (from $130.6 million) for Humanities and $125 million (from $144 million) for Arts. There is reason to believe that the Congress will again resist and that appropriations, when passed, will remain at or near their 1983 levels.

Academic Science

From the viewpoint of academic science, two issues dominated the early months of the Reagan administration: (1) the role of science in the policies and priorities of the administration, and (2) budget decisions affecting the levels of support for various academic science programs.

3. For a summary of the Task Force Report, see *Chronicle of Higher Education,* 23 September 1981, 13ff.

Ever since President Eisenhower institutionalized the office of presidential science advisor, the incumbent of that office has been viewed by the science community, especially the academic science sector, as its voice in the policies of the federal government. Historically, the advisor has been the scientific community's first line of defense in budgetary matters. The role and the influence of the office has varied, of course, with different presidents—very important with Kennedy, less so with Johnson, abolished by Nixon, revived with Ford, quite important with Carter.

Various actions on the part of the Carter White House established a positive context for science in general, and for academic science in particular: the decision to retain the Office of Science and Technology Policy in the executive office; the early appointment of an eminent scientist (Dr. Frank Press of MIT) as director of the Office of Science and Technology policy; and prominent mention of the importance of the role of science in national affairs in State of the Union Messages, in Budget messages and in the Special Message on Science sent to the Congress in March 1979.

In sharp contrast, science policy, in the sense of statements that might indicate President Reagan's position with respect to the role of science and engineering in national affairs, were not forthcoming from the new administration. The concern with which the scientific community viewed this lack of attention was voiced in many quarters and was the subject of an editorial by Dr. Philip Abelson, editor of *Science,* the journal of the American Association for the Advancement of Science. After recognizing the necessity for the administration's short-term actions relating to the economy, the editorial admonished the President:

> For the longer term, if this nation is to enjoy security and to compete economically, it must foster scientific and engineering competence. Of this the Reagan camp seems unaware. The 32,000-word 1980 Republican platform made no mention of medical research. One tiny

paragraph (about 40 words) was devoted to research on renewable energy. Another paragraph (about 50 words) contained the following: "America's technological advantage has always depended upon its interaction with our civilian science and technology sector." A search of the *New York Times* index for pre- or post-election treatment of science or technology by Mr. Reagan drew a blank. During the campaign, substantial efforts were made by publications to elicit information concerning attitudes toward science and engineering. Comments published in the 27 October 1980 issue of *Chemical and Engineering News* were brief and not particularly responsive. The material submitted by the Reagan camp for publication in the October issue of the engineering journal *Spectrum* was an insult to the profession. Some questions were unanswered. Responses were uninformative.

The Reagan camp has so far chosen to ignore the scientific and engineering community. For the short run, it may be able to afford to do so. But for the long term, it can ill afford to lose support among those who advance this nation's technological strength.[4]

What was evident within the new administration (and apparently very difficult for the scientific establishment to accept) was that as science had become just another part of the political stream of events, the president had chosen to treat science policy with the priority he deemed appropriate. He also chose to fill scientific administrative positions with individuals judged to be amenable to his views regarding major priorities and programs and who did not necessarily share the values and priorities of the scientific establishment. Clearly, Mr. Reagan's major priorities had to do with the economic well-being of the country and with defense programs. Major appointments to scientific positions were consequently given low priority and budget decisions regarding the science programs reflected judgments as to how science would best serve to strengthen eco-

4. "President Reagan, Science and Engineering," editorial in *Science*, 29 May 1981.

nomic and defense programs, not how they would best serve
science for the sake of science.[5]

Within the revised budget transmitted to Congress by President Reagan in March 1981, there were significant adjustments
in the funding of scientific research and development programs
for both fiscal 1981 and fiscal 1982. In a special analysis, the
Office of Management and Budget stated that the revisions
were guided "by budget and program priorities and criteria
applied across all Federal programs," including the rebuilding
of the nation's defense capabilities; reduction of economic subsidy programs; and the imposition of fiscal restraint on programs having lower priority than defense and "safety net"
programs.[6]

The application of these priorities and criteria resulted generally in a significant increase in the research and development
programs of the Department of Defense and a significant de-
crease in "civilian" research and development programs, especially programs reflecting an economic subsidy, such as those
in the Departments of Energy and Transportation. The reductions reflected the policy position that the federal government
should limit its role to long-term, high-risk high-potential research and development that the private sector was not likely
to support in the national interest. In addition, the research
and development policy was buttressed by tax policies that
reflected anticipated tax incentives for investment and by reduced burdens of regulation, which hypothetically would encourage civilian research and development.

5. The appointment of the science advisor to the president (who also is head
of the Office of Science and Technology Policy) was not made until late May
1981, after all budgetary revisions were made. The appointee was a little known
physicist, George A. Keyworth, from Los Alamos Laboratory, a government
lab dealing with arms research. In no sense could he be considered a member
of the "scientific establishment."

6. Office of Management and Budget, *Research and Development Revisions
to the Fiscal Year 1981 and 1982 Budgets*. (March 1981), 1. For a general
analysis of the fiscal year 1982 Research and Development Budget see: *New
Directions for Research and Development: Federal Budget 1982*," AAAS Report 6 (Washington, D.C.: American Association for the Advancement of Science, 1981).

Consistent with its policy of fiscal restraint and reducing economic subsidies, the new administration reduced the level of increase proposed by the Carter administration in fiscal 1982 for the National Science Foundation, the Department of Health and Human Services, and for space research. All were considered "clearly inconsistent with the urgent need for fiscal restraint."[7] But the reductions were made with a view to protecting the support of basic research, the basic policy for which, as stated, was aimed at creating long-term stability in funding at lesser rates of increase. The Office of Management and Budget noted that basic research is a "cumulative process," and "gaps created in a period of reduced support cannot be quickly overcome by even sharp increases in basic research spending at a later date."[8]

For universities, particularly private institutions with medical schools whose research programs are supported by significant amounts of federal funds, the Reagan administration's policy as applied to the Department of Health and Human Services, particularly the National Institutes of Health, was of critical importance. As a part of a general policy change whose purpose was to restructure and restrain growth in federal health spending (including health care subsidy through Medicare, Medicaid, the Veterans Administration and Public Health Service hospitals), the 1982 budget revisions included small reductions in the rate of increase in medical research funding for NIH as compared with the Carter budget.

Academic Science: The Special Case of the National Science Foundation

The budget revisions were directed at reducing or eliminating all National Science Foundation research and development programs that were "narrowly focused or relatively less critical to the Foundation's principal responsibilities in the support of research in the natural sciences and engineering that underlies

7. *Research and Development Revisions to the FY 1981 and 1982 Budgets,* 2.
   8. Ibid.

the long-term economic health of the nation. Programs reduced
or eliminated include the support of social, behavioral and economic sciences, science education, and a number of miscel-
laneous programs including intergovernmental, international
and industrial science and technology programs."[9] In addition,
a new initiative in instrumentation upgrading within universities, proposed in the Carter budget, was dropped.

The proposed elimination of the NSF science education program was in keeping with policies that would relinquish much
of the federal government's role in secondary education, particularly programs involving curricular innovation and precollegiate science-teacher development.[10] Although the science
education program has traditionally been the "poor cousin"
of the research-oriented foundation staff and board, the foundation does have a statutory requirement to initiate and support
science education programs at all educational levels.

The National Science Foundation is the second largest supporter of academic science programs. Consequently, the proposed actions on its budget would have had a most significant
impact on science programs in the colleges and universities.
But the proposed reductions, although important in themselves, took on an added and ominous significance because the
Office of Management and Budget, without consultation with
the National Science Board or staff, targeted the cuts largely
toward the social and behavioral sciences, permitting real growth
in engineering and natural science programs. As a result, the
NSF programs in the social and behavioral sciences were tar-

9. Ibid., 5.
10. The Reagan budget revisions essentially eliminated all of the graduate
and postgraduate fellowships (the $9.9 million in fiscal 1982 was intended to
meet existing fellowship commitments); all of the science education research
activities; all development of new materials, methods, and curricula in science;
all faculty improvement programs, including fellowships, the precollege teacher
development program and the Chautauqua-type Short Courses program; all
programs aimed at bringing minorities, women, and handicapped persons into
scientific careers; all undergraduate institutional support programs, including
those in the four-year colleges; all student programs, including undergraduate
research participation and the student science training program; all of the
informal science programs designed for the public and for children, including
support for science museums and television programs.

geted for reduction to a fraction of their size. The impact of these actions on academic research in economics, political science, geography, and sociology would have been especially severe. Also targeted for reduction, although not quite as much as social and economic science, were cognitive and behavioral psychology and anthropology. Reductions of comparable magnitude in federal funding for specific fields of science were unprecedented in the history of the relationship between the federal government and the academic science community, and the shock waves were widely felt.

Following the initial congressional hearings on the foundation's revised budget for fiscal 1982, and in response to a request by one of the members of the authorization committee in the House, the National Science Board issued a statement to explain its role and position in the matter.[11] After recognizing what it described as "the emergency nature of the economic situation and the vigorous remedies the President seeks in the way of Federal expenditure reduction," the board went on to explain that "the emergency precluded the normal process of discussion of program priorities in which the Board could participate meaningfully." The apparent purpose of the remainder of the statement was to let the scientific and academic communities know that the board, too, was distressed by Office of Management and Budget actions and that, through the vehicle of the statement, it was seeking reprogramming authority from Congress.

The statement was somewhat less than convincing in informed quarters and the late Dr. Philip Handler, then president of the National Academy of Sciences, was one of the more vocal critics:

> The heart of the matter lies in the sentence, "It is the Board's statutory responsibility to assist the President by establishing policies and priorities and by guiding the activities of the Foundation to insure that with the available resources, NSF fulfills the functions defined by the

11. *National Science Foundation Budgets for Fiscal Years 1981, 1982, and Beyond,* NSB-81-150, 20 March 1981.

Congress and the goals established by the President in
the most efficient and effective manner possible." Ex-
actly. But their statutory responsibility to establish the
priorities and allocate the resources had, in effect, been
usurped. In not saying so, in unequivocal language, they
may allow this incident to become precedent.[12]

The budget actions regarding the social and behavioral sciences were perceived by many throughout the scientific and
academic communities as being based more upon ideological
considerations than on the merits or shortcomings of the programs themselves. To again quote from the report of the president of the Science Academy:

> The OMB proposals for major reductions in the Na-
> tional Science Foundation budget are particularly trou-
> blesome. It is not the total reduction that is disturbing;
> it is the nature of the individual actions and the manner
> of their doing.
>   The considerable reduction in the program in behav-
> ioral science and . . . the profoundly reduced support of
> social science . . . seems interpretable only as a deliber-
> ate ideological action, for which the overall program of
> general reduction in federal expenditures affords an op-
> portune "cover."[13]

President Handler was equally critical of the administration's
cuts in the foundation's science education program:

> Funding for science education programs is to be termi-
> nated. But the fellowship program, part of the original
> conception of the Science Foundation, has served the
> nation superbly in the years since . . . such a program is
> no less valuable today than at its inception.
>   Yet more serious, in my view, is removing from the
> Foundation the opportunity to contribute to amelioration
> of one of our greater national problems, the decline in
> the general scholastic performance and, particularly, in
> the scientific literacy of those who emerge from our sec-

12. *Annual Report of the President* (Washington, D.C.: National Academy
of Sciences, 28 April 1981), 13–14.
    13. Ibid., 11–12.

ondary school system. This decline is evident in the continuing fall in mean SAT scores; the problem is exacerbated by the large decline in the numbers of very high scores. This suggests that the nation is in danger of losing the future scientific contributions of considerable numbers of intrinsically bright, talented young people who are failing to perform up to their potential. At least equally important, we are inadequately educating young Americans to enter the skilled labor force required in a complex industrial society employing ever more sophisticated technologies. When one contrasts that circumstance with the intense competition of Japanese school life and with the curricular enrichment of secondary schools in the Soviet Union, the matter is cause for great dismay.[14]

Among the actions taken by the academy at the 1981 annual meeting was a resolution strongly supporting the social sciences, not only as worthy of a rightful place in the pantheon of science but also as an enterprise that contributes honorably and usefully to a complex society with increasingly difficult economic and social problems for which we must find satisfactory solutions.

In the weeks following the academy meeting, the social science community, in an effort orchestrated largely by the Consortium of the Social Sciences supplied supporting testimony to the appropriate committees of the Congress, as well as to the public press. The Washington Post, for example, carried a front page article in which it pointed out the irony of an administration which used applied social science techniques and procedures in its political and economic operations and at the same time demolished the very programs that furnished the underlying concepts and data bases that are the roots of those applied programs.[15]

Whether in response to external pressures or because of its own second thoughts after the March budget blitzkrieg is not clear, but in any event, the National Science Board at its annual

14. Ibid., 10–11.
15. *Washington Post,* 29 June 1981, 1.

meeting in June issued a formal statement in support of the social and behavioral sciences. Following several paragraphs in which the statement explained the foundation's historical role in support of science and its chosen role regarding the social and behavioral sciences at this state in their development, it asserted:

> The National Science Board believes that support for social and behavioral sciences, as with all sciences, should continue to be based on criteria of research quality as judged by rigorous critical standards. The Board believes it is imperative to have resources adequate to mount a balanced program. Such a program must include maintenance of large data bases, improvement and strengthening of research methodologies, and provisions of opportunity for innovative investigator initiated projects. The long-range interests of the country require a continuing base of adequate support of the social and behavioral sciences so that the research base and intellectual vitality the United States has established in these fields can be maintained and increased.[16]

However, despite its clear mandate in this area, an analogous statement of support for the equally devastated programs in science education was not forthcoming until after the August meeting of the board, too late for any moral support during the floor debate on the foundation's apropriation.[17]

Academic Science: Targeted Rags to Targeted Riches

Of all the budget and appropriation decisions that affect federally supported research and development programs, none compares in importance for the health and welfare of academic science with those relative to basic research and science education. Not only is basic research the essential business of academic scientists, but of basic research funds available from

16. *Statement on Social and Behavioral Sciences,* NSB-81-288, 17–19 June 1981.
17. *National Science Board's Policy on Science and Engineering Education,* NSB-81-372, 20–21 August 1981.

federal government programs, somewhere between one-half to four-fifths goes to support work within the colleges and universities.

The stringencies facing academic science as a result of the fiscal 1981 and 1982 budget revisions were reinforced by public statements of the president's newly appointed science advisor. At a June 1981 research policy conference sponsored by the American Association for the Advancement of Science, Dr. George Keyworth, while reassuring his audience that the federal government would continue to be the main source of support for basic science, pointed out that the nation would no longer afford to "aspire to primacy across the spectrum of scientific disciplines" and would focus money on "those disciplinary areas where vitality is required to support industrial, military and other essential technologies." In the same setting, the president's chief economic advisor told the conference that, with reference to the administration's general economic "game plan," future years would be "even tougher than fiscal 1982" with controllable budget items being the ones to suffer.[18]

The theme was reiterated in congressional reviews of fiscal 1983 science budgets. Although there was general agreement between President Reagan's science advisor and two of his predecessors regarding the need to strengthen the scientific enterprise, they disagreed on how to do it. Dr. Keyworth told the House Science and Technolgoy Committee that science, like other domestic programs, must share in budget reductions.

I believe the discipline of making such hard choices will ultmately benefit science, just as the occasional pruning of a tree can promote, rather than retard, its health.[19]

Dr. Frank Press, president of the National Academy of Science and former science advisor to President Carter, did not share Dr. Keyworth's enthusiasm for pruning. Instead, he said, government, industry, and academe should make a ten-year

18. "R & D and the New National Agenda" (Sixth Annual AAAS Colloquium on R & D Policy, Shoreham Hotel, Washington, D.C., 25–26 June 1981).

19. As reported in *Chronicle of Higher Education*, 6 January 1982, 13.

"compact" to defend basic research more vigorously and to establish new goals for scientific research.

Like Dr. Press, Dr. H. Guyford Stever, chairman of the Assembly of Engineers of the National Research Council and former science advisor to President Nixon, maintained that serious damage could result from cuts in the federal budget. "It is my thesis that the total government support of research and development is already too low," he said. "A further reduction of it is going to constitute another blow to this important sector."

In a subsequent interview, Dr. Keyworth pursued the theme of eliminating mediocrity in science support programs through the process of the budget, pointing out the difficulty in implementing such a policy because "it represents change and discrimination, and change is always difficult." He added that the "scientific community, as a whole, has been rather oblivious to the requirement for change. They have been used to having generous funds without having to justify in any way, even to themselves, what they are doing with those funds and whether they deserve them. That's where the greatest amount of inertia exists, and that's where the greatest problem is."[20]

As the dust settled following congressional actions on the budgets through fiscal 1983, academic science support fared reasonably well. Agencies and departments whose missions depend heavily upon physical science and engineering experienced increments for basic research, with the Department of Defense playing the most significant part in the overall increase. One item in the defense budget for academic science was aimed at upgrading university research equipment. Funds for basic biomedical research, chiefly from the National Institutes of Health, were marginally increased.

The National Science Foundation emerged from the confused and hectic budget process initiated by the fiscal 1981 revisions in very good shape, especially when compared to the situation proposed by the administration's budget for 1982 as submitted to Congress. For both 1982 and 1983, the Congress added funds to the president's request for NSF, pushing its

20. *Chronicle of Higher Education,* 10 November 1982, 11.

budget beyond the billion dollar level ($1.09 billion) for fiscal year 1983. Major points of difference with the president's proposals were revealed by congressional rejections of administration thrusts to emasculate the social sciences and the science education programs.

With the submission of the 1984 budget to Congress, the themes that had been introduced in prior Reagan administration budgets emerged in bold relief. It was clear from the recommendations that the administration was emphasizing the role of science in a high-technology society—a high-technology society that was giving first priority to its defense establishment. Within the research and development program of the Department of Defense, basic research support was increased by about 13 percent. Collectively, basic research funded by the National Science Foundation, the National Astronautics and Space Administration and the Department of Energy would experience an overall increase of some 15 percent. Within this increment, emphasis was on growth in the physical sciences, with essentially no increase in life science basic research programs, including those of the National Institutes of Health. In a very significant change in course, funds for upgrading laboratory and research equipment in universities were restored. Also included were funds for a shared effort in science education, wherein the Department of Education would support a scholarship program to produce seven thousand mathematics and science teachers per year and the National Science Foundation would support a program for retraining science teachers.

The general theory underlying the administration's science budget for 1984 and its specific relationship to the academic research community was spelled out by Dr. Keyworth in an editorial in *Science:*

> Over the years, in unpredictable, leisurely ways, basic research has led to new technology, which in turn has been the dominant source of growth and of new jobs. But now, in light of what has been happening to the competitiveness of U.S. industries, it is obvious that we cannot simply wait for good things to happen. Science in the universities and the federal laboratories can and

must be better attuned to the opportunities of the industrial world. Our leadership in the international marketplace is at stake.

As a result, our fiscal 1984 program emphasizes selectivity. Increases are targeted to areas likely to have the greatest long-term impacts on new technologies—fields such as mathematics, physics, engineering, plant biology, materials science, astronomy, and space sciences—and specifically to universities, where research involves training people needed in our increasingly technology-dependent economy. In fact, we consider the opportunities so great, and their potential impact so important, that basic research in those fields receives some of the greatest emphasis of any part of the federal budget. . . .

Just as we have not allocated these funds for the usual reasons, we do not expect them to be used in the usual ways. Naturally, the various disciplines would welcome infusions of money to support more projects, say the next 10 or 15 percent of the proposals—all good—that missed the funding cutoff. But the President has not allocated these growth funds to support "next best" research. The real return on this federal investment will come from focusing on the best projects and permitting those nuclei to grow to world-leading concentrations of research excellence. This approach will yield two invaluable products: front-line scientific advances, and a growing body of superbly trained new scientists and engineers.

In spite of its utility, this kind of highly selective approach may not be popular. But science is not on the list of public obligations—like social security or Medicare or veterans' pensions—that have to be funded according to an egalitarian formula. Discretionary spending, which includes all of R & D, makes up only 22 percent of the federal budget today. Every budget item is under intense pressure, and arguments for increases have to be immensely convincing. The fact that so many arguments for research were so persuasive testifies to the central role of research in national policy.[21]

21. Editorial, *Science,* 18 February 1983.

Congressional action on the president's 1984 budget resulted in a reduction in his request for research support within the Department of Defense. Science budgets for nondefense agencies, with few exceptions, resulted in more generous appropriations than requested. Total appropriations for the National Science Foundation rose to $1.32 billion (from $1.09 billion in 1983), with a doubling to $75 million in the allocation for science education. In the debate over NSF appropriations, the old issue of distribution of funds emerged. Representatives of the liberal arts colleges made a strong bid for a "set aside" for funds to be distributed exclusively to these institutions. The Senate failed to support positive House action on the issue, but in the final version of the appropriation bill the foundation was "urged" to reverse the trend in the concentration of its funds and report back to the Congress next year.

Other significant action on nondefense science budgets of particular interest to academic scientists included a rejection by congress of an administration proposal to reduce funds for solar energy research, continued strong support for high-energy physics, protection of space science within universities, and maintenance of NIH research support at essentially current levels.

The increments for basic research in agencies and departments that support primarily physical sciences and engineering, especially the Department of Defense, may be viewed with some discomfort within the academic community. Whether antimilitary attitudes on college and university campuses have changed from those exhibited in the late 1960s and early 1970s is a critical question. That there is a receptive view within the administrations of at least some of the universities was signaled during 1982 budget hearings by the appearance of a delegation of university presidents before the House Armed Services committee, seeking support for the universities they represented. One of the witnesses (President Sproull of Rochester) asserted that "the great crisis of ideology during Vietnam has all but evaporated among faculty, students and staff. There remains one concern: research and training programs on campus must be unclassified because universities must be able to teach and perform research and publish the results in an open environment."[22] But in early February of this year a number of faculty and staff at Stanford University signed a petition objecting to proposed weapons-related research at that university.[23]

Within the academic science community there is undoubtedly agreement with Dr. Keyworth's nonegalitarian approach for the distribution of increased funds for academic science. Whether there is also enthusiasm for his concept of science in the universities being "better attuned" to the opportunities of the industrial world is another matter. The proposed National Advanced Materials Research Laboratory at Berkeley has been proclaimed by the president's science advisor as a perfect example of the administration's approach to improved relationships between government, academic science, and industry. It is to be built in cooperation with industry and, when in operation, will intermingle in some as yet to be determined mode university, government and industrial scientists.

We have been witnessing, of course, a new set of relationships between some of the research universities and the business world as a result of developments in biomedical research. These relationships involve patent ownership and the production and marketing of research discoveries in "bioengineering." They offer both high rewards and high stress because of the relatively large sums of money that frequently result from successful marketing and licensing ventures in the pharmaceutical industry. The role of faculty members who pursue this kind of research and who become involved with commercial developments of their research products, either through established corporations or by establishing their own companies while remaining faculty members, is central to the problem. Whether the university as an institution should become involved as a "silent partner" is also part of the issue. As yet there are only a few institutions exploiting such arrangements,

22. "DOD Funds More Research in Universities," *Science*, 29 May 1981, 1003. The presidents were Richard A. Atkinson, chancellor, University of Calif., San Diego; Robert L. Sproull, president, University of Rochester; John Wright, president, University of Alabama at Huntsville.

23. *Stanford Observor*, February 1983, 4.

but the influence of these few is being widely felt as a result of faculty pressure to adopt such policies elsewhere. Faculty recruitment will be influenced in those academic areas subject to such practices. One wonders, witnessing these developments and thinking of Dr. Keyworth's idea, how universities so involved will cope with the problem of faculty hearts being where considerable treasure is also.

On balance, it appears likely that federal budgets supporting academic science will be maintained under the Reagan administration, although they will lean heavily in the direction of the physical sciences. Although the projected increments for basic research are substantially mixed and may not ideally fit the needs of the academic scientific community, they do suggest that the concept of basic research, at least in the natural sciences, seems to be recognized by the administration as something of value. Also of significance in administration actions is the fact that in matters pertaining to the academic science budgets, the National Science Board has clearly demonstrated that it is no longer a source of independent strength for the academic science community.[24] From the fiscal 1982 budget to the pronouncements of administration strategy for science budgets in fiscal 1984, it is obvious, in the words of former NSB Chairman Walker, that control of national science policies, including academic science policy, has shifted from the scientific community to the bureaucracy.

24. For a comprehensive review of the National Science Board, see Committee on Science and Technology, House of Representatives, *The National Science Board: Science Policy and Management for the National Science Foundation, 1968–1980*. (Washington, D.C.: U.S. Government Printing Office, 1983).

5

The Reagan Administration
and
Regulatory Reform

In his book *Scholars, Dollars and Bureaucrats*, Chester Finn states that "the single most controversial element of higher education policy in the late 1970s, surpassing in intensity the fractious disputes over financial assistance to students and institutions" is the extent to which government regulations began to intrude on the affairs of higher education.[1] The Republican platform, taking note of the regulatory expansion of the previous Democratic administration, had promised to "hold the federal bureaucracy accountable for its harassment of colleges and universities and clear away the tangle of regulation that has unconscionably driven up their expenses and tuitions."[2] As an indication of the high priority he assigned to the issue of regulatory reform, President Reagan, very early after taking office, formed the Presidential Task Force on Regulatory Relief and placed it under the direction of Vice-President Bush.[3]

In commenting upon the approach to be taken by the task force, Vice-President Bush observed that the regulations, generally speaking, needed examination in order to determine whether they exceeded the legal requirements upon which they were based and to see if broad performance standards might not appropriately replace the tight specifications that many of

1. Chester E. Finn, Jr., *Scholars, Dollars, and Bureaucrats* (Washington, D.C.: Brookings Institution, 1978), 140–41ff.
2. "The Party Platform," *Change* 12, no. 6 (September 1980): 47–53.
3. For an excellent discussion of the general problem of deregulation, see William G. Colman, "Intergovernmental Deregulation: Requisite for a Viable Federalism," *National Civic Review,* (January 1983: 24–35).

the regulations imposed upon government contractors and funds recipients.

In response to a request from the task force, the American Council on Education forwarded to Mr. Bush a document outlining the modifications that colleges and universities would like to see made in rules and regulations affecting them. Among the priority items indicated by the council's request were Circular A-21, which determines indirect costs on federal grants and contracts; regulations for enforcing Executive Order 11246, which bars bias by recipients of federal contracts; regulations dealing with Title 9 of the Education Amendments of 1972, which bars sex bias in federally assisted educational programs; rules for carrying out a law barring bias against handicapped students, section 504 of the Rehabilitation Act of 1973; various Veterans Administration rules concerning GI Bill benefits; and rules of the Environmental Protection Agency for disposal of hazardous waste.[4]

At the 1981 annual meeting of the National Association of College and University Attorneys, Secretary Bell indicated that the administration would be granting more authority to colleges and universities "to regulate themselves." He also stated that the Department of Education would change its style of enforcing rules, doing more to avoid court action. With reference to previous administration practices, Mr. Bell observed that the Office of Civil Rights had a tendency to send out "letters of findings" too precipitously, charging colleges and universities with not complying with federal regulations before they had a reasonable chance to comply. It was the secretary's hope "to modify our behavior so that you won't have reason to get angry quite so often."[5]

The case for easing the "burden" of federal government regulation has, of course, been made many times and in many ways.[6] It is entirely reasonable, on the one hand, to ask that

4. For further details, see *Chronicle of Higher Education,* 11 May 1981, 10.

5. *Chronicle of Higher Education*, 6 July 1981, 1.

6. See, for example, Carol Van Alstyne and Sharon L. Coldren, *The Costs of Implementing Federally Mandated Social Programs at Colleges and Universities* (Washington, D.C.: American Council on Eucation, 1976). The general case is made reasonably objectively in *The Entangling Web* (Washington, D.C.: Editorial Projects for Education, 1979).

regulatory aims and purposes be administered with a sensitivity and understanding of the character of the entity being regulated. On the other hand, it is unreasonable to seek essential exemption to regulation, especially while enjoying the benefits of publicly sponsored programs. In the case of colleges and universities, there is a tendency to overmake the case, with reference to both administrative rules and regulations as well as with reference to regulations that stem from social legislation.

In a study of government-university relations in the administrative sphere, the National Commission on Research pointed out that the central issue producing the greatest difficulty in the fiscal-administrative area is accountability.[7] The government, in order to assure the citizenry that the best efforts are produced and that public funds are not being wasted, is anxious to attain its program objectives and fulfill its stewardship responsibilities to the taxpayer. However, the universities also want to conduct their activities in their traditional manner, avoid what they perceive as unnecessary administrative requirements, and protect the integrity of their institutions.

The origins of the problems are deep-seated. They include procedural and organizational differences between universities and government, as well as differences between university operations and private enterprise, where the applications of fiscal and administrative accountability tools were principally developed. The heterogenous character of our institutions of higher learning creates extremely diverse conditions. Obviously, researchers and institutions alike should be expected to meet the highest standards of honesty and prudence. But there also is an inherent requirement for some flexibility in meeting standards. The dominant research support distribution system of project grants, however commendable, does not fit the way research is conducted; finite periods of support do not relate to the continuous nature of research inquiries. Further problems arise from the competition for scarce funds, which requires that research proposals be increasingly specific,

7. "Accountability: Restoring the Quality of the Partnership," in *Report of the National Commission on Research* (Washington, D.C., 1980). See also *Science,* 14 March 1980, 1177–82.

notwithstanding the great uncertainty of the research process. Rising indirect costs and the revision of federal principles that govern their reimbursement leave many problems unsolved. These continuing disagreements derive primarily from the erosion of a mutual but largely unwritten understanding of the basic nature of the government-university relationship in support of research.

The commission's report leads one to conclude that fault is distributed about equally in the erosion of administrative relationships between government and the universities. Perhaps the most striking observation the commission made is that despite the fact that a close relationship has existed for the better part of a half century, ignorance and misunderstanding about the nature and behavior of the other partner is profound and pervasive on both sides. Such ignorance and misunderstanding extend from fundamental principles to the most trivial elements of behavior and inevitably cripple efforts to bring about improvements in the relationship. In the commission's view, neither the government nor the universities now do an adequate job of assuring that their policymakers and operating agents understand properly the complex system within which they work. The essence of the recommended actions to relieve the tensions that mark the administrative-regulatory area is that the government and the universities seek new ways to inform and educate themselves and their constituencies about each other in all matters relating to government-university programs. What is needed is a "bridging process" through which the two parties might see the relationship as a whole and get it back on a more productive track. The recommended instrument, suggested as a five-year experiment, is an

independent forum whose purpose would be to watch over the university-government research relationship and to guide its evolution.

Such a forum should provide a non-adversarial setting. Here persons from the public, Congress, universities, and the federal agencies would address the major policy issues and problems in the research associations between the universities and the government. They would derive effective responses in terms of the objectives of the relationship and its overall role in the national research enterprise.

If convened by a highly respected non-governmental or quasi-governmental organization or by a private foundation with a strong interest in the national research enterprise, perhaps such a forum could accomplish what present structures have been unable to do.[8]

Whatever degree of success may be attained by the Reagan administration's review of administrative regulations, federal regulations stemming from social legislation involve problems of a vastly more fundamental nature. In Finn's discussion of the impact of social legislation and the regulations and executive orders stemming from it, he points out that it is from these sources that the most invidious intrusions into the affairs of the colleges and universities are to be found. However, in considering federal regulations in this sphere, Finn states:

every single one of those regulations, procedures, forms and lawsuits can be traced to a law (or executive order) that was enacted in response to constituent pressure, and those constituencies now monitor the performance of the government enforcers with fierce dedication and single minded enthusiasm. The bureaucrats are not to be blamed, except perhaps for occasional excess or whimsey in interpreting the law. It is the lawmakers who are responsible, but they acted in order to help or appease groups that sought changes. Hence anyone who seeks to mitigate the effects of government regulation on colleges and universities had best recognize at the outset that it is not a struggle between the academy and bureaucracy, but between parts of the society that want change and parts that resist changing.[9]

It may well be that one should recognize the clash of differing views within the society and that, over the long run, the values

---

8. Ibid. 1182. The "forum" idea is recommended also by the National Academy of Sciences report, *Strengthening the Government-University Partnership in Science,* April 1983.

9. Finn, *Scholars, Dollars, and Bureaucrats,* 140.

of a society, especially a democratic society, will be determined
in some more or less rational interaction among differing views.
But to assume that the interpretation and administration of laws
passed by Congress are to be by "government enforcers" whose
performance is measured by their response to selected constituencies who exhibit "fierce dedication and single minded
enthusiasm" raises a serious question about the proper role
and responsibilities of executive branch officers of government,
all of whom have taken an oath of office that is intended to
ensure equitable interpretation and administration of law for
all parties. This is the question that led to the Reagan platform
promise to "hold the federal bureaucracy accountable" for
what was perceived as the harassment of colleges and universities, as well as other institutions in the private sector.

But just as with the administrative rules and regulations, so
in the interactions between the academy and the bureaucracy
in the administration of regulations stemming from social legislation, the shortcomings have not all been on the side of the
federal government. There is little doubt that there has been
an unwarranted extension of bureaucratic power into the affairs
of the colleges and universities. But many colleges and universities have too often taken hesitant stands.[10] It seems almost
as if in defending themselves as institutions with certain inalienable rights, they automatically assume a posture of opposing the rights that the social legislation is intended to assure
for others. One gets the feeling that these institutions believe
that to preserve their fundamental purposes and to set the
highest standards for higher learning is somehow to do violence
to basic concepts of equity, fairness, compassion, or justice
for those who seek and participate in higher education. There
is a clear and understandable difference between bigotry or
bias in such fundamental matters as these on the one hand and,
on the other, questioning the validity of the concept of "goals

10. See especially Lamphere v. Brown University, C.A. no. 75–0140, United
States District Court for the District of Rhode Island, 12 September 1977. See
also Rajender et al. v. University of Minnesota, C.A. no. 4-73-435, United
States District Court for the District of Minnesota, August 1980.

and timetables'' or in pointing out the incongruity between
"nondiscrimination" as mandated in the social legislation and
"nondiscrimination" as defined by the representatives of an
overzealous regulatory body.

At the same time, there is no validity to the frequently heard
recital that because they are, in some almost mystical fashion,
different from other institutions within society, colleges and
universities ought to be exempt from the requirements of social
legislation. Obviously government has the obligation to determine compliance with the law. But the circumstances of legal
oversight, its procedures, and its evaluative tools must be fash-
ioned with a respect and an understanding of the institutions
that the laws were meant to govern. The proposition that in
such matters as which faculty to employ, what problems to
pursue, which students to admit, and what curriculum should
be taught, colleges and universities are more appropriate judges
than the federal government, on the basis of either substantive
qualification or assigned authority, is the main issue.

However enthusiastic the Reagan administration may be with
respect to regulatory reform, there is no reason to believe that
it will have a better understanding than previous administrations of the purposes, aims, methods, and procedures of universities. It is not that government is inherently nefarious; it
is simply that government is not the academy, and the academy
is not government. Although both may have purposes that put
the public interest foremost, these purposes are not congruent
and they may even at times be in conflict. It is up to the
universities to make clear to the government what their purposes are and what conditions for interrelationships are acceptable. These actions on the part of the universities will more
expeditiously assure proper regulations, either administrative
or those stemming from social legislation, than will party platform statements, or even Presidential Task Forces on Regulatory Relief.

6

Prospectus

Dean Acheson once observed that popular conceptions about government are in large part interesting folklore, and that the instinct of the bureaucracy for self-preservation along with the egotism of bureau chiefs perpetuates it. One of these bits of folklore "is that policy originates at the top and is passed down." To be sure, great decisions, Mr. Acheson held, "are, for the most part, made at the top, when they are not made by events. But as for policy—the sum total of many decisions—it must be said, as it has been said of sovereignty, that its real sources are undiscoverable. One fact, however, is clear to anyone with experience in government, the springs of policy bubble up; they do not trickle down."[1]

There is much evidence to support Mr. Acheson's observation as one reviews federal higher education and academic science programs since World War II in a search for systematic policy or some pattern or principle that sets the course for government in its affairs with higher education. In those instances when there is explicit policy, it appears to be based essentially on political or temporal interests that reflect someone's or some group's wisdom, prudence, or expedience. There is the nagging thought that perhaps the concept of a comprehensive policy for higher education and academic science programs may be a convenient construct around which one may

1. *New York Times Magazine,* 11 October 1959, 86.

design seminars or write staff papers, but otherwise it is a mirage. It may be that any expectation of achieving such a goal within the complexity that marks our form of political democracy is simply tilting at intellectual windmills.

The rarity with which clearly formulated comprehensive policy in any area of responsibility is articulated by the federal government is in large measure a function of the fact that within the executive branch, especially when the policy in question affects programs in a number of executive branch agencies, the president is the only individual who can pronounce policy. One does not expend presidential pronouncements frequently. But, when the president is sufficiently concerned with a given issue, a policy will emerge.

Mr. Reagan's concern with what he perceives as "the economic crisis facing America" has been proclaimed from the early days of the presidential campaign of 1980, and has been reiterated in his various messages to the Congress, particularly in the fiscal year 1982 budget revisions.[2] Whether or not one considers his "Economic Plan" and the directly related "Budget Reduction Plan" as being a statement of economic policy, it has been the dominating influence guiding administration priorities and program decisions in all areas, including higher education.

By midterm in the Reagan administration, "events" as well as Congress have intruded to modify administration policies.[3] This is most strikingly evident in the displacement of promised balanced budgets by continuing deficits, but it is also very apparent in higher education programs. As we have noted, strong bipartisan congressional forces have been unwilling to

2. *1982 Budget Revisions,* 1–10.

3. Although it is beyond the scope of this paper, an interesting question is whether the strength of the president's expressed economic policy may have been eroded by the overwhelming success of his confrontation with the Congress in the fiscal 1981 budget revisions and the 1982 budget. The devastating defeat dealt the Democratically controlled House in 1980 may have led to an over-optimistic interpretation of the president's "mandate," consequently leading to the adoption of a political posture too far to the "right" on the liberal-conservative dimension. The counteractions of the Congress and the midterm elections are evidence to support the argument that the early victory over Congress contained the seeds of later failures.

accept administration recommendations for cuts of the severity desired by the president. Thus as the time approaches for hearings which will serve as a basis for the Higher Education Amendments of 1985, Congress has emerged as essentially an equal partner to the president in setting the directions for future federal support of the higher education enterprise. The important question for higher education is whether it can present an effective case for inclusion on a national agenda which is already crowded with problems of the economy, the national defense and various social issues.

Senator Moynihan in a cogent, albeit somewhat bitter essay has expressed serious doubt that this is now possible.[4] He feels that it was possible in the period between 1957 and 1972 for the universities to have "negotiated a distinctive relationship between themselves and the national government [and] that this was not done involved a profound failure of leadership." The university community is now in such a state of dependency that it is not able to deal effectively with Washington. In Senator Moynihan's view, higher education has taken such a sharp drop on the political agenda of the nation that its support has become simply a routine function of the federal government, striving to retain its share of the budget while becoming involved in a process of "tireless tinkering" with program components.

There have been a number of statements and actions emanating from the higher education community and its Washington representatives since the installation of the Reagan administration which may furnish evidence to test Moynihan's hypothesis regarding the ability of higher education to negotiate a healthy relationship with the federal government. More or less in response to the new administration, the American Council on Education in conjunction with other presidential-level higher education associations established a National Commission on Higher Education Issues. The commission, composed of forty-five educational leaders, was charged with looking at the overall context of higher education and making "specific

4. Daniel P. Moynihan, "State vs. Academe," *Harpers* 261 (December 1980): 33.

recommendations" on "specific problems" to "specific groups" capable of doing something about them. Robben W. Fleming, president of the Corporation for Public Broadcasting and former president of the University of Michigan, stated in the news release announcing his chairmanship of the commission: "This is not a study commission. Our goal is not to publish a five-pound report, file it on a bookshelf and go out of business. We want our recommendations put to work on campuses, in government and elsewhere."[5]

In a follow-up essay of his analysis of the future of education's "liberal consensus," Chester Finn has expressed his view that as a function of the Reagan administration's profound changes in the basic assumptions that have undergirded social and educational policies of the federal government, the time has come to form a new national consensus whose unifying idea is educational quality.[6] Among the precepts that define the essence of the proposed consensus are a prescribed body of knowledge to be mastered, the measurement of student progress by performance, improved quality of teacher personnel, deregulation of educational institutions, a commitment to research, and vigorous national debate on the mission and content of higher education.

In what has become a traditional "shopping list," the American Council on Education, speaking as "the major coordinating body for higher education" and "representing the concerns of its constituency," has forwarded its Higher Education Agenda to the Ninety-eighth Congress.[7] On the assumption that congressional priorities will be devoted to legislation aimed at reducing unemployment, stimulating the economy, and to questions of national defense, the council outlines the "community's priorities" as follows:

5. "The National Commission on Higher Education Issues," *Change* 13, no. 7 (October 1981): 51; "To Strengthen Quality in Higher Education," *Educational Record* 64, no. 3 (Summer 1983): 18–19.

6. Chester E. Finn, Jr., "Toward a New Consensus," *Change* 13, no. 6 (September 1981): 16ff.

7. *A Higher Education Agenda for the 98th Congress* (Washington, D.C.: American Council on Education, 1983).

1. To maintain federal student assistance programs to assure the fullest development of the nation's human resources.
2. To strengthen the research enterprise for scientific and technological advancement.
3. To introduce tax incentives that encourage charitable giving, research and development, and savings for educational purposes.
4. To renovate higher education's decaying physical plant, including laboratory instrumentation, technology, and facilities as part of the effort to rebuild the nation's infrastructure.
5. To establish regulatory mechanisms that provide accountability without unnecessary bureaucratic control and that minimize diversion from the central task of education.
6. To support categorical programs addressing high-priority national and international purposes.

The lead sentence of the memorandum urges the Congress as it "addresses priority legislation . . . to bear in mind how closely these objectives are linked to the capacities of America's colleges and universities." In describing in more detail this linkage, one gets an impression that the justification for relationships between the federal government and higher education has retrogressed to the instrumentality concepts of pre-1965. Perhaps the authors of the memorandum feel that this is the only line of argument that will be persuasive under conditions that currently define political reality. But the line between political reality and political expediency frequently gets blurred in the environment of Washington and the tone of the "Agenda" must be viewed as evidence in support of Senator Moynihan's position.[8]

Whether one is inclined to view the relationships between the federal government and higher education as being formu-

8. In Senator Moynihan's previously cited piece he makes a characteristically telling point which bears importantly upon the problem of higher education's relationship with the federal government. "Sometimes, outside interests capture a federal government bureaucracy. May it simply be noted that 37.8 percent of the budget of the American Council on Education in 1979 came from federal funds" (p. 40).

lated and driven through consensus, as something which can now only be maintained on a basis of political considerations, or with sanguinity, there should be little doubt in anyone's mind that these relationships are now strikingly different from those which marked the period immediately following World War II. In that period, a highly productive partnership was struck between the federal government and higher education. Both institutions shared a concern for matters affecting the welfare of the nation. Both expressed this concern in a desire to protect the autonomy while strengthening the intellectual bases, first of science, and later of the full spectrum of higher learning. With time the relationship became one of confrontation, marked by intrusions on the part of the federal government and by heightened suspicions of both partners. With the election of President Reagan, we have moved into another period of change, introducing a new era in matters of political economy and social policy. Higher education, along with other institutions within the society, must sort out its values and determine its course under these new conditions.

In making a successful match between its own values and those of the current or any future federal administration, as a first step, it is necessary for those responsible for the future of higher education to develop an understanding with those responsible for the future of the nation that there is a mutual need for each other, and that the need requires a long-term, systematic commitment if the welfare of the nation is to be enhanced. The commitment carries with it an understanding that however imperfect institutions of higher learning may be perceived as being, government must recognize the validity of their autonomy and their purposes. Their purposes, however supportive of government, are not the purposes of government. At the same time, those responsible for higher education must also recognize its purposes and be willing to defend them and the standards that are necessary to attain them, even at the risk of dissolving all relationships with the federal government. To do otherwise risks becoming simply an instrument of the federal government.